BEARDED DRAGON FOR KIDS

LEARN TO CARE FOR, FEED,
AND ENJOY YOUR NEW REPTILE FRIEND

FINN RYLANCE

GRAPEVINE BOOKS

Published by

GRAPEVINE BOOKS

www.grapevinebooks.com

email: contact@grapevinebooks.com

Ordering Information:

Quantity sales: Special discounts are available on quantity purchases by corporations, associations, and others.

For details, reach out to the publisher.

First published by Grapevine Books, 2025

Contents

Get Your Free E-book

Get Your Free E-book
Scan the QR code below to instantly access the e-book **'The Ultimate Bearded Dragon Trivia Challenge'**, absolutely free

SCAN ME

https://bonus.grapevinebooks.com/bearded-trivia-challenge

Part 1
Introduction to Bearded Dragons

Chapter 1
The First Encounter

It started with a flick of a tongue and a slow blink. I hadn't planned on bringing home a dragon that day. I was simply tagging along with a friend to the pet store, mostly to pass time, not to adopt a scaly companion. The rows of colorful fish tanks and chirping parakeets did little to hold my attention. I wandered aimlessly—until I came face to face with a creature that looked like it had wandered straight out of a medieval fairytale and into a terrarium.

There it was, basking under a heat lamp with a regal calm, resting on a piece of driftwood like it owned the place. Its scales shimmered in soft shades of gold and sand, and its triangular head looked like it had been sculpted from ancient stone. A beard of spiky scales framed its face, giving it an almost wise, wizard-like expression. I crouched down, intrigued. That's when it happened—those dark, curious eyes locked with mine.

There was no rush, no fear, no frantic scrabbling to hide in the corners. It tilted its head slowly, almost comically, as if it were trying to understand what sort of creature *I* was. Then came the slow, deliberate arm wave—a common behavior I would later learn was a submissive greeting. At the time, I thought it was saying hello.

I laughed. Not the kind of laugh you give when something's merely amusing, but the kind that bubbles up from being genuinely caught off guard by joy. There was something absurdly charming about this miniature dinosaur. He wasn't trying to be cute or playful like a puppy—he didn't need to. He was simply himself: calm, proud, and unbothered.

I asked a staff member what this little guy was. "Bearded dragon," she replied, as if it were the most obvious thing in the world. She explained their temperament, their needs, their lifespan, their odd little quirks. I listened, but my mind was already made up. I was smitten.

That afternoon, I walked out with a terrarium, a bag of crickets, and a dragon I named Darwin. And just like that, my world expanded. I had no idea how much this tiny reptile would teach me about patience, trust, and the quiet, steady kind of companionship.

This book is for anyone curious about bearded dragons—whether you're considering one as a pet or just want to understand what makes them so beloved. Because once you meet a dragon, it's hard not to fall under their spell.

Chapter 2
What Is a Bearded Dragon?

A bearded dragon is a type of lizard known for its gentle demeanor, spiky appearance, and curious personality. Native to the arid regions of Australia, this reptile has become one of the most popular exotic pets in the world. The name "bearded dragon" comes from the distinctive beard-like flap of skin under its chin, which it can puff out and darken when feeling threatened, excited, or dominant. While the display might look intimidating, most of the time these creatures are surprisingly docile and friendly.

Scientifically known as *Pogona*, bearded dragons belong to a group of reptiles called agamid lizards. There are eight recognized species, but the most commonly kept as a pet is *Pogona vitticeps*, also known as the central bearded dragon. This species thrives in warm, dry environments like deserts, shrublands, and woodlands. Their natural habitat is filled with rocky outcrops, fallen branches, and open spaces—features that pet owners often try to replicate in home enclosures.

Bearded dragons are medium-sized reptiles, typically growing to about 18 to 24 inches in length from head to tail. Their body is covered in rough, scale-like skin with rows of spines along the sides and under the throat, adding to their dragon-like appearance. Despite their somewhat fierce look, they are known for their calm nature and often tolerate handling well. In fact, many owners report that their bearded dragons enjoy perching on shoulders or resting in laps.

These reptiles are diurnal, which means they are active during the day and sleep at night, just like humans. They love basking under a heat lamp or the sun, soaking up warmth and light. Their habits are easy to observe and enjoyable to interact with, making them great companions for people who are new to reptile care.

One of the most fascinating traits of bearded dragons is their body language. They communicate using gestures like head bobs, slow arm waves, and changes in color. For instance, a male might bob his head quickly to assert dominance, while a female might wave an arm in submission. Their coloration can shift slightly based on mood, temperature, or stress. Watching these subtle behaviors helps owners better understand and bond with their pet.

Bearded dragons are omnivores, meaning they eat both plants and animals. Their diet includes leafy greens, vegetables, and a variety of insects. They require a balanced intake of protein, calcium, and vitamins to remain healthy. With proper care, bearded dragons can live for 8 to 12 years in captivity, and some even longer.

More than just a pet, a bearded dragon is a creature of instinct, warmth, and quiet wisdom. They are a small window into the reptilian world, and they offer companionship in a way that is unique, peaceful, and often surprisingly affectionate. Whether basking, exploring, or simply sitting still, a bearded dragon has a presence that draws people in. Understanding what a bearded dragon is helps us appreciate not only their biology but their quiet charm and deep connection to the natural world.

Chapter 3
Natural Habitat and Origins (Australia's deserts)

Where Bearded Dragons Come From

Bearded dragons are native to Australia, where they thrive in some of the continent's harshest and driest environments. Most notably, the central bearded dragon (*Pogona vitticeps*), the most commonly kept species as a pet, hails from the arid interior—an expanse of red sands, rocky plains, and dry scrubland that stretches across parts of Queensland, New South Wales, South Australia, and the Northern Territory. Other species of *Pogona* inhabit different regions, including woodlands and coastal zones, but all are well-adapted to the challenging Australian climate.

These reptiles evolved in isolation, as Australia's vast, unique ecosystems provided an ideal environment for their development. While many animals around the world might struggle with such demanding conditions, bearded dragons are perfectly suited for life in places where daytime temperatures can soar above 100 degrees Fahrenheit and water sources are scarce.

Australia's deserts are not empty, lifeless places. They're teeming with resilient flora and fauna, from eucalyptus shrubs and spinifex grasses to insects, lizards, and birds. Bearded dragons are one of the more visible and iconic inhabitants, often seen basking on rocks or slowly meandering across open spaces in search of food.

Life in the Australian Outback

The outback is a term often used to describe the remote and rugged parts of inland Australia, and for bearded dragons, it is both home and fortress. These deserts and semi-arid woodlands are characterized by intense sunlight, sudden temperature drops at night, and very little rainfall. Vegetation is sparse, with low bushes, hardy grasses, and scattered trees. The soil is often sandy or rocky, perfect for digging shallow burrows.

Within this landscape, bearded dragons exhibit remarkable adaptability. They are masters at conserving energy and moisture. Their body temperature is regulated externally, so they begin their day by basking in the morning sun to warm up. Once their muscles are active, they forage for insects, nibble on leaves and flowers, or scout their territory. As the day grows hotter, they retreat to shaded areas or burrows to avoid overheating.

This daily rhythm, dictated entirely by the environment, shows how deeply in sync bearded dragons are with their surroundings. Their behavior and biology have evolved in tandem with the land, making them one of the outback's most successful reptiles.

Adapting to Harsh Environments

Surviving in such an extreme setting requires special adaptations, and bearded dragons have plenty. Their flat, broad bodies allow for efficient heat absorption while also helping them flatten against surfaces to avoid detection. The spiny scales along their sides and beard may look intimidating, but they serve a purpose: when threatened, the dragon can puff out its throat, making itself appear larger and more formidable to predators.

Their coloration blends well with the dusty reds, browns, and tans of the desert floor, offering camouflage that protects them from birds of prey, dingoes, and larger reptiles. Unlike animals that rely on speed to escape danger, bearded dragons use stillness and disguise to avoid detection.

Another remarkable feature is their ability to extract moisture from their food. Since water is limited in the wild, bearded dragons rely on insects, dew, and plant matter to stay hydrated. They can also go long periods without drinking if necessary, thanks to highly efficient kidneys that conserve fluids.

In short, the natural habitat of bearded dragons is a land of extremes, and their bodies are built to meet every challenge it presents. Their ability to adapt and thrive in such a demanding environment is a testament to the evolutionary marvels of the Australian outback. Understanding where these creatures come from helps us better appreciate the intelligence and resilience hidden behind their calm eyes and gentle movements.

Shelters and Hiding Spots in the Wild

Despite their dragon-like name and rugged appearance, bearded dragons are not aggressive creatures. In the wild, they spend much of their time avoiding confrontation. Survival often depends on having the right hiding spots. The Australian outback may look barren to the untrained eye, but it provides a variety of natural shelters that bearded dragons make full use of.

Rocks, fallen tree limbs, and crevices are among the most commonly used shelters. During the hottest part of the day, bearded dragons will retreat to these shaded, cooler spots to avoid overheating. Many will dig shallow burrows beneath the roots of shrubs or into loose soil to create a safe, temperature-regulated refuge. These burrows not only shield them from the sun, but also offer protection from predators like snakes, birds of prey, and goannas.

The ability to find and utilize these hiding spots is key to their daily rhythm. Bearded dragons are keen observers of their environment. They learn where to retreat when danger approaches and often use the same safe zones repeatedly. These shelters also serve as nighttime dens, helping them conserve body heat and stay out of sight after dark. Unlike mammals that may construct permanent nests, bearded dragons adapt to what is available, showing their flexibility in making a home from the landscape around them.

Daytime Creatures: Diurnal Lifestyle

Bearded dragons are diurnal, meaning they are active during the day and sleep at night. This sets them apart from many other reptiles that are crepuscular or nocturnal. In their natural setting, a bearded dragon's day begins with the sun. At sunrise, they climb to a high rock or log to bask in the warm light. This is crucial for warming their cold-blooded bodies, which rely on external heat to become active.

As the morning progresses and their muscles reach the right temperature, bearded dragons begin their hunt for food. Their activity peaks during the mid-morning hours when it is warm but not dangerously hot. They patrol their territory for insects, nibble on desert vegetation, or simply observe their surroundings. These reptiles are naturally curious, often turning their heads and shifting positions to get a better view of movement nearby.

As midday approaches and temperatures rise sharply, activity slows. Bearded dragons then seek shelter in shade or burrows, conserving energy during the hottest hours. This midday break is an important part of their behavior and helps prevent heat stress. Later in the afternoon, they may emerge again briefly to explore or eat before retreating for the night.

This diurnal lifestyle makes them easier for people to observe and interact with. Their active hours align with ours, and their behavior throughout the day reflects a deep connection to the sun's rhythm. This pattern is not just instinctual—it is a carefully evolved response to living in one of the world's toughest climates.

The Role of Sun and Heat

The sun is everything to a bearded dragon. In the wild, sunlight is not just a source of warmth; it is the trigger for many biological processes that are essential to their survival. Bearded dragons use the sun to regulate their body temperature, a behavior known as thermoregulation. In the morning, they position themselves to absorb maximum heat. You may see them flatten their bodies to increase surface area or darken their skin to absorb more light efficiently.

Thermoregulation controls nearly every aspect of their daily routine. Digestion, for example, is directly linked to body temperature. Without sufficient heat, a bearded dragon cannot properly digest its food, which can lead to serious health problems. Activity levels, breeding behavior, and even mood are influenced by how warm their environment is.

In addition to heat, bearded dragons require ultraviolet B (UVB) light. In their natural habitat, this comes from direct exposure to the sun's rays. UVB is crucial for the synthesis of vitamin D3, which allows their bodies to absorb calcium from their diet. Without it, they are at risk of metabolic bone disease, a debilitating condition that weakens their skeletal system.

The relationship between bearded dragons and the sun is one of nature's most finely tuned partnerships. It explains why proper lighting is one of the most important aspects of caring for them in captivity. In the wild, the sun dictates everything from what they eat to when they rest. Their internal rhythms are wired to the rise and fall of sunlight, a connection that has guided them for millions of years across the harsh beauty of the Australian outback.

Natural Diet in the Wild

In their native Australian habitats, bearded dragons have access to a diverse but unpredictable menu. They are true omnivores, meaning their diet includes both animal and plant matter. What they eat depends on availability, age, season, and environment. Insects like crickets, beetles, grasshoppers, and ants form a large part of their protein intake. These are hunted actively, with bursts of surprising speed and precision.

Bearded dragons are visual hunters. They rely on sharp eyesight to spot movement in their surroundings. When they detect a bug, they freeze, lock in, and strike with their sticky, fast-moving tongue. Insects offer not just protein but also hydration—essential in desert environments where standing water is rare.

Plant matter also plays a significant role. Wild bearded dragons graze on a variety of desert plants including flowers, leaves, fruits, and even seeds. Edible vegetation provides fiber, nutrients, and moisture. Some of their favorite snacks include dandelions, mulberry leaves, clover, and native blooms. This helps them balance their diet naturally and supports digestion and overall health.

In times of scarcity, they adapt quickly. They may eat smaller prey, dig for roots, or fast for extended periods without serious harm. Their ability to adjust to fluctuations in food availability is key to their survival in the wild. Unlike in captivity, where meals are predictable and scheduled, wild bearded dragons eat opportunistically, taking advantage of whatever is present in their ecosystem.

Predators and Survival Tactics

Though they are skilled at blending into their environment, bearded dragons are not immune to danger. In the wild, they must constantly be alert for predators, especially during their more vulnerable moments—while basking, foraging, or moving across open terrain. Their list of enemies includes birds of prey like hawks and falcons, snakes, dingoes, monitor lizards, and even large spiders.

To defend themselves, bearded dragons rely heavily on camouflage and behavior rather than aggression. Their earthy-toned bodies match the colors of sand, stone, and dry foliage, allowing them to remain hidden from view. When still, they often look like nothing more than a lump of bark or a patch of dirt.

When spotted, their first response is usually to flee. They can run with surprising speed in short bursts and will often bolt toward cover. If escape is not possible, they employ a different set of tactics. Puffing up their bodies, flaring their beards, and darkening their color can make them look larger and more threatening. Some will even hiss and open their mouths wide to show the dark interior, a visual threat display meant to intimidate.

Occasionally, they use bluffing strategies. The slow arm wave, which signals submission during social interactions, can also be used to confuse or de-escalate a confrontation. If absolutely necessary, a bearded dragon may bite, but this is rare and only used when all other defenses fail.

Survival is also helped by their keen senses. They are acutely aware of vibrations in the ground, which alert them to approaching threats. Their lateral eyes offer a wide field of vision, allowing them to spot predators from multiple angles without needing to move. These sensory advantages, combined with behavioral defenses, make them well-equipped to navigate a world full of danger.

Seasonal Changes and Brumation

Though Australia is known for its heat, it does experience seasonal shifts—especially in the interior where bearded dragons live. Winter in the outback brings cooler temperatures and reduced daylight, both of which trigger a physiological response in bearded dragons known as brumation. This is similar to hibernation in mammals but is not quite the same.

During brumation, a bearded dragon's activity slows dramatically. They eat less, move infrequently, and often spend weeks or even months in a dormant state. Their metabolism slows, and they enter a period of energy conservation. In the wild, they retreat into burrows or shaded crevices, avoiding the cold and reducing their exposure to predators.

Brumation is crucial for survival during times when food is scarce and conditions are not ideal for digestion or mobility. It also plays a role in their reproductive cycle. Many dragons emerge from brumation with increased hormonal activity, signaling the start of the breeding season.

For young or juvenile dragons, brumation may not occur at all, or it may be shorter and less intense. Each individual follows their own rhythm, guided by cues in temperature and light.

This seasonal pattern demonstrates how closely tied bearded dragons are to their environment. Their bodies and behaviors adjust in harmony with nature's cycles, allowing them to thrive in a place where the balance between life and survival is delicate. Understanding these rhythms helps us appreciate the complexity behind the calm eyes of these remarkable reptiles.

Chapter 4
Species and Types of Bearded Dragons

By now, you've come to see that bearded dragons are remarkable creatures—resilient, intelligent, and surprisingly expressive. But did you know there isn't just one type of bearded dragon? In fact, eight different species fall under the *Pogona* genus. Each species comes with its own temperament, size, and even quirks in behavior or appearance. While only one or two of these species are typically kept as pets, getting to know the broader family gives you a deeper understanding of where your dragon fits into the bigger picture.

You might never encounter some of these species in a pet store or rescue center, but learning about them offers a glimpse into how incredibly adaptable these lizards really are. Let's explore the range of bearded dragons across Australia and how they differ from one another.

Meet the Broader Bearded Dragon Family

If you already live with a bearded dragon—or are considering adopting one—it's almost certain you're dealing with *Pogona vitticeps*, the Central Bearded Dragon. But *vitticeps* has relatives, and while they may not be lounging in your local reptile shop, they're thriving in different corners of Australia's diverse ecosystems.

Some are more reclusive, others are smaller, and a few are extremely rare and protected by law. Understanding this wider family will not only help you appreciate the complexity of your own bearded dragon, but may even influence how you observe or care for them.

The Quiet Cousin: Lawson's Dragon

You may occasionally come across *Pogona henrylawsoni*, also known as Rankin's or Lawson's dragon. If you're working with limited space or prefer a smaller reptile, this might be the species for you. They're less than half the size of a standard *vitticeps*, but their personality is just as captivating.

Lawson's dragons tend to be more skittish at first but can become quite tame with consistent handling. Because of their smaller size, they don't require large enclosures, making them more manageable for apartment living or beginner keepers. If you ever want to branch out but still enjoy the company of a bearded dragon, *henrylawsoni* could be your next step.

The Oversized Wildcard: Eastern Bearded Dragon

Now, picture a larger, darker version of the dragon you know, one that's a bit moodier and not particularly fond of being handled. That's the Eastern Bearded Dragon (*Pogona barbata*), and it's more common in the wild than in homes.

Though they look quite similar to *vitticeps*, Eastern bearded dragons often exhibit bolder behavior and a quicker temper. If you were to see one in the wild, especially along Australia's eastern coastline, you'd notice their more intense beard displays and slightly rougher look.

It's best to leave this species to its natural environment. While they're fascinating to observe, they don't typically adapt well to captivity, especially compared to their more laid-back central cousins.

The Desert Specialists

Among the lesser-known species are three variations of *Pogona minor*: *minor minor*, *mitchelli*, and *minima*. These lizards tend to live in drier, more rugged parts of Western Australia and the northern regions of the continent.

If you enjoy reptile research or ever plan to see bearded dragons in their native habitats, these are the kinds of dragons you'd likely need binoculars and a lot of patience to spot. They're smaller than *vitticeps*, more slender, and often more secretive.

One standout here is Mitchell's Bearded Dragon (*Pogona minor mitchelli*), which features a longer tail and an even more elusive personality. It's rarely seen even by Australians. If you find yourself hiking through the Kimberley region or peeking under shrubs on the western coast, you might be lucky enough to catch a glimpse.

The Island Dwarfs and Hidden Rarities

If you love the idea of miniatures, meet *Pogona minor minima*, a tiny, island-dwelling species found on the Abrolhos Islands. These are true dwarfs, growing only to around 8 or 9 inches in length. They've adapted to island life and are a brilliant example of how isolation shapes evolution. You won't find them for sale, though—they're strictly protected and studied primarily by scientists.

Even smaller is *Pogona microlepidota*, the most mysterious of all. Found in the Drysdale River National Park, this species is barely larger than your hand and is so rarely seen that much of what we know about it comes from occasional field sightings and museum specimens. It's safe to say that this species is best admired from afar, both physically and legally.

What About Pet Breeds and Morphs?

If you're shopping for a bearded dragon or already have one, you may hear the term "morph" tossed around. These are not different species but rather different **color and scale variations** of *Pogona vitticeps*, created through selective breeding.

Think of morphs as different "styles" rather than separate species. Some morphs have more vivid colors—like citrus orange, fire red, or snow white—while others may have smoother skin (such as the Leatherback morph) or translucent skin that gives their eyes a ghostly look.

Breeders have created dozens of morphs, and while they don't usually change the dragon's behavior, they may require slight differences in care. For example, a translucent morph may be more sensitive to light, and a scaleless "Silkie" morph may need extra humidity and protection from abrasions.

If you're considering a morph, ask yourself whether you're prepared to meet its specific needs. Also remember that extreme morphs, while beautiful, sometimes come with genetic weaknesses. When in doubt, prioritize health and temperament over looks.

Why Species Knowledge Is Important

You don't need to memorize every Latin name or track down every species in the wild. But having a general awareness of the types of bearded dragons gives you context. It helps you understand your pet's behavior, anatomy, and habitat preferences on a broader level.

Let's say your dragon shows a particularly intense black beard or tends to be more skittish than others. Knowing that certain traits exist in wild relatives can help you see these behaviors not as oddities but as variations rooted in evolution.

It also helps you make informed choices. If you're ever tempted to adopt a dragon labeled as "exotic" or "rare," understanding the difference between species and morphs ensures you're not taking on something you can't properly care for.

In Summary

Bearded dragons come in many forms, from the classic *vitticeps* lounging on basking rocks across Australia's deserts to tiny, elusive species hidden in island caves or thick brush. Whether you're caring for a pet, admiring a dragon at a zoo, or reading up for the sheer fascination of it, knowing these types deepens your appreciation.

Your dragon is part of a larger story—one that stretches across deserts, coasts, and forests, shaped by climate, terrain, and time. And now, you're part of that story too.

Chapter 5
Bearded Dragons as Pets Popularity and Appeal

When people think of adopting a pet, they often imagine wagging tails, purring cats, or colorful birds. But over the past few decades, a new contender has quietly risen in popularity: the bearded dragon. If you've ever seen one basking under a warm light, calmly observing the world with ancient-looking eyes, you've probably wondered what it's like to own one. As it turns out, there's a reason bearded dragons have become one of the most beloved reptiles in the pet world.

In this chapter, you'll explore what makes these scaly companions so appealing—from their gentle temperament to their manageable care requirements. Whether you're already a bearded dragon parent or simply curious about what the fuss is about, you'll see why more and more households are opening their hearts (and terrariums) to these modern-day mini dinosaurs.

The Rise in Popularity

Bearded dragons were once virtually unknown outside their native Australia. Their export became restricted in the 1960s and 70s, but before the ban, a small number had been exported to the United States and Europe. Captive breeding programs took root, and slowly but steadily, the bearded dragon found its way into the pet trade.

What happened next was nothing short of a reptilian revolution. Breeders discovered that these lizards were not only easy to reproduce in captivity, but also far more tolerant of handling than many other reptiles. Over time, selective breeding produced a range of color variations and morphs, further increasing their appeal. Today, *Pogona vitticeps*, the central bearded dragon, is one of the most commonly kept pet reptiles in the world.

You'll find them featured in YouTube videos, Instagram reels, and even classroom science corners. They've become a fixture in pet stores, animal rescue centers, and reptile expos. So what's the secret to their success?

A Calm, Friendly Disposition

If you've ever held a bearded dragon, you know what sets them apart from other reptiles right away: they're calm. While snakes may coil defensively or geckos dart for cover, a well-socialized bearded dragon will often just relax on your hand—or even your shoulder—without fuss. They tolerate handling well and rarely bite unless they feel threatened or startled.

Their laid-back attitude makes them excellent companions for children (with adult supervision) and for first-time reptile owners. They're not demanding, they don't hiss or hide constantly, and they're often content just sitting with you while you read, watch TV, or work at your desk.

This gentle nature doesn't just make them easy to care for—it also fosters a genuine emotional bond between you and your dragon. They might not wag their tail or jump into your lap, but they do learn to recognize your face, your voice, and your routines. Many bearded dragon owners report that their pets greet them in the morning or crawl toward them at feeding time, forming what feels like a quiet but meaningful relationship.

Manageable Size and Needs

Another reason bearded dragons are so popular is that they strike the perfect balance between "impressive" and "manageable." Adult dragons typically grow to about 18 to

24 inches long, making them large enough to be visually striking, but not so big that they require a room-sized enclosure or pose a risk to other pets.

Their needs are relatively straightforward: a properly sized terrarium (at least 40 gallons for an adult), a basking lamp, UVB lighting, clean substrate, and a diet of insects and vegetables. Once you've set up their habitat, daily care consists of feeding, misting or bathing occasionally, spot-cleaning, and spending some time interacting with them.

Unlike mammals, they don't require walks, litter boxes, or grooming appointments. They're quiet, they don't shed fur or trigger allergies, and they won't tear up your couch or chew your shoes. This makes them a great option for people with limited space, sensitive allergies, or unpredictable schedules.

Fun to Watch and Interact With

Bearded dragons aren't just passive pets that sit around all day. They have a range of behaviors that are both fascinating and endearing. If you spend time observing your dragon, you'll notice head bobs, arm waves, color changes, basking rituals, and curious little tilts of the head as they examine the world around them.

Feeding time can be particularly entertaining. Watching your dragon hunt live insects like crickets or dubia roaches can be like watching a nature documentary in real-time. Some dragons even learn to associate their owners with food and will eagerly run toward you when they see you coming.

With enough consistency, many bearded dragons can be "trained" to respond to routine. Some learn to climb onto a hand when presented, recognize feeding tongs, or even follow finger movements. A few particularly social individuals will happily ride around on their owner's shoulder or explore a safe, enclosed space outside their tank.

Low Noise, Low Drama

If you live in a small apartment or shared space, you'll appreciate how quiet a bearded dragon is. They don't bark, chirp, or squawk. They won't keep you up at night or disturb your neighbors. The only sounds you're likely to hear are the rustling of their claws as they move or the soft crunch of a cricket during feeding.

They're also low-drama. While all animals need care and attention, bearded dragons are not particularly prone to sudden mood swings or unpredictable aggression. With a stable environment and regular interaction, they tend to remain steady and predictable.

This stability makes them ideal for people who want a meaningful pet experience without the constant maintenance or emotional intensity that some other pets demand.

A Gateway to Reptile Keeping

For many people, bearded dragons are the first step into a larger fascination with reptiles and exotic animals. Once you've learned how to care for a bearded dragon, you may feel more confident exploring other species, from geckos and skinks to snakes or even amphibians.

Because they are relatively forgiving pets—as long as you do your research and meet their basic needs—bearded dragons help you build the habits and knowledge necessary for more advanced reptile care. Their popularity has led to a wealth of accessible resources, forums, care sheets, and even online communities where you can learn, share, and connect with other dragon keepers.

Great for All Ages

Bearded dragons make excellent companions for a wide range of people. Children are drawn to their dinosaur-like appearance and their interactive behavior. Adults appreciate their independence and calm energy. Seniors often find comfort in the routine of caring for a dragon without the physical demands of walking or grooming a larger animal.

They also serve as educational pets. Many schools and science programs use bearded dragons to teach students about reptile anatomy, desert ecosystems, and responsible animal care. Their visual appeal, combined with their approachable nature, makes them perfect ambassadors for the reptile world.

Emotional Benefits of Dragon Companionship

Finally, and perhaps most surprisingly, bearded dragons can offer emotional comfort. Their steady presence, gentle behavior, and subtle forms of interaction create a calming effect. For people dealing with anxiety, loneliness, or stress, the simple act of watching a bearded dragon bask or feeding them by hand can be deeply soothing.

You may find that your dragon becomes a quiet anchor in your day—a reason to slow down, observe, and engage with a creature that, while silent, brings a peaceful rhythm to your home. There's something grounding about the way bearded dragons live: simple, present, and unhurried. It's a way of being that many of us can learn from.

Conclusion: The Appeal That Lasts

It's easy to understand why bearded dragons continue to capture the hearts of so many. They're beautiful to look at, easy to care for, and full of personality. They don't ask for much, but they offer a lot in return—companionship, curiosity, and a quiet kind of joy that stays with you.

Whether you're drawn to their ancient appearance, their manageable lifestyle, or the bond you can form with them over time, one thing is certain: having a bearded dragon in your life is a unique and rewarding experience. And once you've gotten to know one, it's hard to imagine not having that calm little face watching you from across the room.

Part 2
Anatomy & Physical Features

Chapter 6
Unique Features of the Bearded Dragon

One look at a bearded dragon and it's clear why these reptiles stand out. With their spiky exteriors, dinosaur-like gait, and iconic "beard," they look like something out of a fantasy novel. But beyond appearances, their body is filled with fascinating adaptations and features that serve important purposes. Whether you're a proud bearded dragon owner or just curious about these gentle reptiles, getting familiar with their unique anatomy will help you better understand their behavior, health, and needs.

This chapter takes you through the key physical traits that make bearded dragons such captivating creatures—from their namesake beard to their tails, toes, eyes, and more.

The Famous Beard

The most iconic feature of a bearded dragon is, of course, the beard itself. Located under the chin, this flap of skin can puff out and darken, creating a striking display. Both males and females can do this, though males tend to do it more often and more dramatically.

You might see a beard puff up in different situations. It can be a defense mechanism, a response to stress, a sign of excitement, or a signal during social interactions like courtship or territorial disputes. When your dragon feels threatened or tries to appear more dominant, it will flare out its beard, making it look bigger and more intimidating. At the same time, the beard may turn jet black—an even stronger visual warning.

If your dragon is puffing its beard during handling or when a new object enters its space, it might be feeling uncertain or defensive. On the other hand, some dragons puff their beards during a good stretch, almost like yawning. Once you learn to read the context, the beard becomes a helpful window into your pet's mood.

Tail: A Balancing Tool and Energy Reserve

The tail of a bearded dragon is more than just a decorative extension. It plays a key role in balance, movement, and even survival. When your dragon runs or climbs, it uses the tail as a stabilizer. It shifts position to counterbalance the body, allowing smoother movement and preventing falls.

In the wild, bearded dragons also use their tails to store fat. In captivity, a well-fed dragon often has a plump tail base—an indicator of good health and nutrition. If the tail starts to look thin or bony, it may signal illness or malnutrition.

Unlike some other lizards, bearded dragons do not regenerate their tails if they lose them. This is important to know, especially if you have other pets in the home. Their tails are strong but not invincible, and rough handling can lead to injury.

You may also notice a dramatic curl in the tail when your dragon is basking or feeling alert. This curled posture often reflects a state of excitement or heightened awareness. It's a quirky little feature, but one that many owners find endearing.

Scales and Spikes: More Than Decoration

At first glance, the rough, spiky texture of a bearded dragon's body may seem intimidating. But despite appearances, these scales aren't sharp or dangerous. They're actually quite soft to the touch—especially once your dragon is used to being handled.

The "spikes" that run along the sides of their head, throat, and body serve multiple functions. First, they're a visual defense. When threatened, a dragon will puff up its body, making the spikes stand out and giving the illusion of a larger, tougher creature. This can be enough to deter predators in the wild or signal dominance in social settings.

The scales also provide some degree of physical protection from rough terrain and predators. While not armor in the traditional sense, they do act as a buffer, especially around sensitive areas like the limbs and flanks.

Color-wise, the scales help with camouflage and temperature regulation. In their natural habitat, dragons blend in with the sand, rocks, and brush. They can slightly adjust their skin tone depending on heat or stress. A darker color absorbs more heat and is common during cold mornings or brumation. A lighter tone helps them stay cool and is often seen during hotter periods.

Eyes and Eyelids: Designed for Observation

Bearded dragons have excellent eyesight. Their wide-set eyes give them a broad field of vision, allowing them to spot movement from multiple directions. They rely heavily on sight to locate food, detect predators, and observe their environment.

Their eyelids can close, giving them the ability to blink and keep their eyes moist. They also have a clear third eyelid called the *nictitating membrane*. This translucent layer can sweep across the eye to clean and protect it while still allowing some vision. You might catch a glimpse of it during blinking or when they're exposed to bright light or dust.

Many dragons will engage in slow, deliberate eye movements—often turning their heads to fixate on something that caught their attention. Whether it's a feeder insect, your hand, or a shadow on the wall, this tracking behavior shows just how visually attuned they are.

Tongue and Teeth: Tools for Feeding

The bearded dragon's tongue is long, sticky, and fast. When hunting, they shoot it out to capture prey like crickets or worms. The sticky surface ensures a good grip, while the quick motion helps with accuracy. In the wild, this quick strike method allows them to catch moving insects before they can escape.

Their teeth are small and arranged in rows along the upper and lower jaws. They don't have sharp fangs like predators, but their teeth are strong enough to crush insect shells and chew plant matter. Young dragons may bite more often as they explore their environment, but adults typically become more controlled and gentle.

If you look closely, you might notice that their jaws are quite powerful. This allows them to eat tougher food items like hard-shelled beetles or fibrous vegetables.

Limbs and Claws: Built for Climbing and Digging

Each of your dragon's four limbs ends in five clawed toes. These claws are built for traction, climbing, and digging. In the wild, dragons often scale branches or rocks to bask and survey their surroundings. They also dig to create burrows for brumation or egg-laying.

In captivity, you'll see similar instincts. Your dragon might dig at the corner of its enclosure, scratch at soft substrate, or attempt to climb decor or the walls of the tank. These behaviors are natural and often healthy.

The limbs themselves are strong and slightly splayed, giving the dragon a sturdy, low-to-the-ground stance. This helps them remain stable on rough surfaces and gives them a bit of that "prehistoric" gait that makes them so visually striking.

Nostrils and Breathing

Bearded dragons breathe through nostrils located near the top of their snout. Their respiration is usually quiet and steady. If you notice open-mouth breathing during basking, it's likely just a way to regulate internal temperature.

However, if the breathing seems labored or noisy, or if mucus is present, it could indicate a respiratory infection. Being aware of what normal breathing looks and sounds like helps you catch problems early.

Ears: Hidden but Functional

You may not notice their ears right away, but bearded dragons do have external ear openings on the sides of their heads. These small round holes are not covered by flaps or skin, but they're quite sensitive. Dragons can detect low-frequency sounds and vibrations, which helps them stay alert in the wild.

Sudden loud noises may startle your dragon, and repeated disturbances could cause stress. Speaking gently and approaching slowly shows respect for their sensitive hearing and helps build trust.

Conclusion: Built for Survival and Adaptability

Bearded dragons are beautifully engineered by nature. Every feature—from their beard to their tail, from their spines to their scales—serves a purpose. These traits have helped them thrive in the harsh environments of the Australian outback and adapt remarkably well to life in human homes.

As a pet owner, understanding these unique features gives you better insight into your dragon's world. The more you know about how their bodies work, the better you can care for them, bond with them, and appreciate the quiet brilliance hidden beneath those ancient-looking eyes.

Chapter 7
Color Morphs and Patterns

When you imagine a bearded dragon, you likely picture earthy tones—tan, brown, and sandy gold, perfect for blending into desert rocks and dirt. These colors are typical of wild bearded dragons, especially the species *Pogona vitticeps*. But in captivity, breeders have discovered something extraordinary: with selective breeding, bearded dragons can exhibit an incredible variety of colors, patterns, and even scale textures that do not occur in nature. These are called morphs.

If you've spent time browsing bearded dragons online or at expos, you've probably noticed dragons in bright red, pale white, lemon yellow, and even lavender hues. Some are smooth-skinned, while others have bold stripes or translucent skin. Understanding these morphs can be both exciting and useful, especially if you're considering adding a dragon to your home. In this chapter, you'll explore what color morphs are, how they're created, what patterns exist, and what it means for the care and selection of a pet bearded dragon.

What Are Color Morphs?

A color morph is a variation in color, pattern, or scale texture that occurs through selective breeding. These morphs are not separate species—they're all part of *Pogona vitticeps*—but they represent different genetic traits passed down through generations.

In the wild, natural selection favors muted, camouflaged colors that help dragons hide from predators and absorb heat effectively. In captivity, however, breeders began noticing and encouraging unusual colors by pairing dragons with distinct appearances. Over time, this led to the development of consistent lines of dragons with unique colors, smooth or altered scales, and new visual patterns. These traits are now well-known among reptile enthusiasts and are a major part of the bearded dragon trade.

Some morphs are primarily color-based (like Citrus or Red morphs), others are about scale texture (like Leatherback or Silkback), and some are eye-catching combinations of both.

Common Color Morphs

1. Citrus

This morph typically features vibrant yellow and lime green tones. Citrus dragons are eye-catching and appear almost neon under certain lighting. They are often mixed with hypo or translucent traits to further brighten their appearance.

2. Red

Red morphs range from soft peach to deep blood red. These dragons are particularly striking when combined with orange undertones and a high-saturation pattern. Deeper reds tend to be more sought after and are often more expensive.

3. Orange

Orange dragons are bold and warm in tone, sometimes appearing like glowing embers. This morph can be quite variable, sometimes overlapping with red or yellow hues depending on the breeding pair.

4. Sandfire

One of the original designer morphs, Sandfires were developed for their rich gold, orange, and rust colors. They were among the first morphs to gain popularity in the 1990s and paved the way for more complex lines.

5. Yellow

These morphs appear sunny and bright, often with pale underbellies and golden highlights along the back and limbs. They're cheerful-looking dragons and often paired with hypo genes to enhance brightness.

6. White and Snow

These dragons have a pale appearance, ranging from light silver to off-white or beige. They're often called "Snow" morphs and can have cool, muted patterns that give them a frosty or ghostly look.

7. Lavender and Purple

True purple is rare, but lavender tones exist in some lines. These are subtle hues that appear more clearly during juvenile stages and often fade with age. However, in combination with translucent genes, the lavender morph can retain more of its pastel appearance.

8. Blue

While "blue" morphs are commonly advertised, they are often more of a grayish tone or appear blue under certain lighting due to translucent skin. A true blue bearded dragon is extremely rare and usually refers to a hint of blue around the belly or sides.

Pattern Variations

In addition to color, morphs can also express different patterns on their scales. These patterns are determined by the distribution of pigment and the texture of the scales.

1. Striped (Tiger)

These dragons have dark bands running across their backs and sometimes down the tail. The stripes can be bold or faint and may contrast dramatically with the base color.

2. Hypo (Hypomelanistic)

Hypo dragons lack some of the dark melanin pigment, giving them a softer, pastel-like appearance. Their nails are often clear or pale instead of black. Hypo is not a color in itself but rather a trait that lightens the dragon's overall appearance. Many color morphs are enhanced when combined with the hypo trait.

3. Translucent (Trans)

Translucent dragons have semi-transparent skin and darker eyes that may appear black or purple. Hatchlings often look glossy and jelly-like, though their color matures over time. Their bellies can be see-through when young. When combined with bright color morphs, the translucent gene creates a very surreal, glowing appearance.

4. Leatherback

This morph features reduced scale size and texture, resulting in a smoother, flatter appearance. The reduced scaling allows colors to appear more vibrant and saturated. Leatherbacks still retain some spikiness on the head and sides but are noticeably smoother than standard dragons.

5. Silkback (Silkie)

Silkbacks have no spikes or textured scales at all. Their skin is completely smooth and almost slippery to the touch. Because they lack natural protection, they require higher humidity and more careful handling to avoid abrasions. Silkies often display incredibly vivid colors but need experienced keepers.

6. Dunner

Named after the breeder Kevin Dunn, this morph affects scale direction and body shape. Dunners often have more chaotic patterns, circular tail markings, and even reversed scale growth. They tend to look a little "messy," but their uniqueness is part of their charm.

7. Zero

The Zero morph lacks visible pattern and color, appearing almost solid white or gray. These dragons look minimalistic and are sometimes compared to albinos, though they retain normal eye color. They're striking in their simplicity and often very popular.

8. Witblits

Witblits are similar to Zeros but may have soft, muted color tones like cream or beige. They also lack strong patterning but are not as stark as Zeros. The word "Witblits" means "white lightning" in Afrikaans, a nod to their pale appearance.

Why Morphs Matter for You

If you're considering a bearded dragon as a pet, you may be drawn to a specific color or pattern. Morphs offer a chance to find a dragon that visually resonates with you. However, it's important not to choose based on appearance alone.

Some morphs, like Silkbacks and Translucents, can come with extra care requirements.

Silkies are prone to skin damage and dehydration. Translucent dragons may be more light-sensitive or have weakened immune systems if not bred carefully.

When shopping for a morph, be sure to research not just the look but the health history of the breeder and the dragon's parents. Ethical breeders will prioritize strong genetics, good health, and responsible care over flashy colors alone.

The Morph Market and Pricing

Bearded dragons with rare or highly saturated morphs can be more expensive. While a standard dragon may cost between $50 and $100, a unique morph—especially if it's a Zero, Dunner, or combination morph—can sell for $200 to $1000 or more.

Prices reflect rarity, color intensity, scale type, and breeder reputation. However, high cost doesn't always equal better quality. A healthy standard morph with good temperament and strong genetics may bring you just as much joy as an expensive dragon with flashy looks.

Conclusion: A World of Color and Character

Color morphs and patterns add a whole new layer of appreciation to bearded dragons. They allow for personal expression, variety, and fascination in the reptile-keeping world. Whether you choose a fire-red Leatherback, a snowy Zero, or a standard earthy-toned dragon, each one is unique in personality and charm.

Morphs highlight just how diverse and beautiful *Pogona vitticeps* can be. But behind every morph is a living creature that depends on you for care, comfort, and companionship. Choose wisely, care deeply, and enjoy the beauty your dragon brings—whether it glows in gold, shimmers in lavender, or simply smiles in sandy tan.

Chapter 8
Growth Stages – From Hatchling to Adult

Watching a bearded dragon grow is one of the most rewarding parts of keeping one as a pet. From the moment it hatches, this tiny lizard goes through several fascinating stages, each with its own care requirements, behaviors, and milestones. Understanding how your bearded dragon develops over time will help you give it the best possible environment at each step.

In this chapter, you'll explore the key growth stages of a bearded dragon—from fragile hatchling to mature adult—and learn what to expect as your dragon transforms into its full-sized, confident self.

Stage 1: Hatchling (0 to 2 Months Old)

Hatchlings are typically about 3 to 4 inches long when they first emerge from their eggs. At this stage, they are delicate, fast, and incredibly curious. Their skin is soft, their colors are usually more vibrant than in later life, and their movements are quick and reactive.

In the wild, hatchlings are extremely vulnerable to predators, so they rely on their speed and instincts to survive. In captivity, your job is to provide a secure and nurturing setup to help them thrive.

Key Needs:

- **Tank size:** A 20-gallon tank is usually sufficient for the first few weeks.
- **Temperature:** Basking spot around 105–110°F; cool side around 80°F.
- **UVB lighting:** Essential for calcium absorption and bone growth.
- **Diet:** Primarily insects—tiny crickets, fruit flies, or pinhead roaches—offered

multiple times daily. Some finely chopped greens can be introduced but may be ignored early on.

- **Handling:** Keep it minimal. Let them get used to their environment first.

At this age, growth is rapid. Hatchlings can double in size within a month if properly fed and kept warm. You'll likely notice frequent shedding as their bodies outgrow their delicate skin.

Stage 2: Juvenile (2 to 6 Months Old)

By now, your dragon should be between 6 to 12 inches long and starting to develop a sturdier body and more defined features. This is one of the most active and demanding stages in terms of food and energy.

Juveniles are often extremely alert, curious, and a little skittish. They begin to recognize routines, respond to feeding times, and may show the first signs of social behavior, such as head bobbing or arm waving—even if no other dragons are present.

Key Needs:

- **Tank size:** A 40-gallon breeder tank is recommended at this point.
- **Diet:** Insects still make up about 70 to 80% of the diet. Feedings can be reduced to 2–3 times per day. Begin offering more variety in greens such as collard, mustard, and dandelion.
- **Calcium supplement:** Dust insects daily with calcium powder.
- **Shedding:** Expect frequent shedding, especially around the limbs and tail.
- **Handling:** Gradually increase. Use gentle, slow movements to build trust.

Juvenile dragons are fun to watch but require patience. They may climb more, dig, and even try to scale the tank walls. Their personalities also begin to emerge during this stage.

Stage 3: Sub-Adult (6 to 12 Months Old)

This is the adolescent stage. Your dragon will be growing rapidly, typically reaching 14 to 18 inches or more depending on genetics and diet. Their growth will start to slow down slightly after the 8-month mark, but they still need plenty of nutrition and interaction.

You may notice some behavioral shifts—males might start showing territorial behavior, while females may become slightly more reserved. This stage is also when sexual dimorphism becomes easier to identify. Males usually develop broader heads, more pronounced femoral pores, and thicker tails.

Key Needs:

- **Tank size:** At least 50–75 gallons, especially if nearing adult size.
- **Diet:** Begin shifting the ratio to 50% insects and 50% greens.
- **Behavior:** Some dragons may go through a phase of "bratty" behavior—hissing, refusing food, or becoming fussy with handling. This usually passes with consistent care.
- **UVB and basking:** Still essential for development.

This is a great time to strengthen your bond. Daily interaction, hand-feeding, and short, supervised outings help your dragon build confidence.

Stage 4: Adult (12 Months and Up)

Most bearded dragons reach adulthood by their first birthday, though some continue to grow slowly into their second year. An adult dragon typically measures between 18 to

24 inches and has a more muscular, filled-out body. Their coloring may become richer or more muted, and their behavior tends to become calmer and more predictable.

Key Needs:

- **Tank size:** A full-grown adult needs at least a 75-gallon enclosure, though larger is always better.

- **Diet:** Shift the balance to about 70–80% greens and vegetables, with insects as supplements a few times per week.

- **Feeding frequency:** Adults typically eat once a day or every other day.

- **Handling:** Most adult dragons enjoy lounging on their keeper's shoulder or lap. They are usually easy to handle and rarely bite if treated respectfully.

Adult dragons may become less active but still benefit from regular enrichment. Safe objects to climb, areas to explore, and time outside their tank help keep them mentally stimulated.

Shedding and Growth Milestones

Shedding is a natural part of your dragon's growth at every stage, though it slows down in adulthood. Juveniles may shed in patches or whole-body molts every few weeks, while adults might shed just their tail or limbs a few times a year.

Always provide gentle misting and warm baths during shedding to help loosen dead skin. Never pull off stuck shed—this can damage the new scales underneath.

Understanding Growth Variation

Not all dragons grow at the same rate. Factors such as genetics, diet, lighting, enclosure size, and even stress levels can affect growth. Some dragons stay on the smaller side despite ideal conditions, while others grow quickly and reach adult size by 10 months.

Tracking your dragon's weight and length every few weeks during the first year can help you catch early signs of stunted growth or health concerns.

Conclusion: The Journey of Growing Up

Watching your bearded dragon grow from a tiny, wide-eyed hatchling into a calm and confident adult is a remarkable experience. Each stage comes with its joys and challenges, but all offer opportunities to learn and connect more deeply with your pet.

By understanding these growth phases, you'll be better prepared to care for your dragon's changing needs, offer appropriate food and habitat, and build a lasting bond. Growth isn't just about size—it's about transformation, trust, and companionship. And through it all, your dragon will remind you that great things often come in scaly, sun-loving packages.

Chapter 9
Vision, Smell, and Senses

Bearded dragons might not speak our language, but they interact with the world in incredibly sophisticated ways. Their survival in Australia's rugged landscape has depended on an acute awareness of their surroundings. As a result, their senses—particularly vision, smell, and sensitivity to vibration—are surprisingly advanced. Understanding how your bearded dragon perceives the world can help you interpret its behavior, provide better care, and build a stronger relationship with your pet.

Let's explore how bearded dragons see, smell, and sense the world around them.

Exceptional Eyesight

Sight is arguably a bearded dragon's strongest sense. In the wild, their survival depends on spotting predators and prey from a distance. In captivity, you'll quickly notice how your dragon uses visual cues to make sense of its environment.

Bearded dragons have large, laterally placed eyes that offer a wide field of view. This gives them excellent peripheral vision, making it easier to detect movement from nearly all directions. They can focus quickly and track moving objects with precision—a skill that helps them hunt live insects with astonishing accuracy.

They can also see in color, including ultraviolet (UV) light. This UV vision is especially interesting because it helps them detect subtle patterns on other dragons that are invisible to the human eye. These UV-reflective signals may play a role in communication, mating, or dominance displays. It also explains why UVB lighting is not just a health necessity, but potentially a part of how they perceive the world visually.

You may notice your dragon tilting its head when looking at something. This head tilt helps improve depth perception and allows it to better judge distance before pouncing on prey or stepping onto a new surface. It's one of the more charming and intelligent-looking behaviors bearded dragons display.

The Mysterious Third Eye

Bearded dragons possess a unique feature called a **parietal eye**, often referred to as a "third eye." This is not a functioning eye in the way you might imagine, but rather a light-sensitive organ located on the top of the head between the eyes. It's visible as a small, grayish scale.

The parietal eye can detect changes in light and shadow, particularly from above. This is helpful for detecting aerial predators like hawks or other large birds. In captivity, it helps them stay oriented to the natural day-night cycle and may play a role in regulating circadian rhythms.

Sudden changes in overhead lighting or shadows can startle your dragon—this is why some dragons seem nervous when a hand moves quickly above them. Their instinct tells them something might be swooping down. It's best to approach your dragon from the front or side, where its primary eyes can see you clearly.

Smell and the Jacobson's Organ

Although sight is dominant, bearded dragons also use their sense of smell to explore and interpret their world. Their method of "smelling" isn't exactly like ours—it's a combination of sniffing through the nostrils and analyzing particles with an organ called the **Jacobson's organ** or **vomeronasal organ**, located in the roof of the mouth.

You'll often see your dragon flicking its tongue across surfaces or into the air. This action collects scent particles, which are transferred to the Jacobson's organ when the tongue retracts. It's the same behavior seen in snakes and some other reptiles.

This sense allows your dragon to recognize food, identify other reptiles, and even become familiar with your scent. Some dragons will lick your fingers or clothing not as a sign of affection, but as a way to gather information about you. Over time, this familiar scent may become a source of comfort and security.

Hearing and Vibration Sensitivity

While bearded dragons have visible ear openings on either side of their heads, their hearing is more attuned to low-frequency sounds and ground vibrations than high-pitched noise. Their ability to detect subtle vibrations is a critical survival tool in the wild, where approaching predators or scurrying prey may give away their position through movement rather than sound.

In a home environment, this means that heavy footsteps, dropped objects, or slamming doors can be startling. Even music or television with heavy bass can cause agitation. Try to observe how your dragon reacts to the sounds in your space, and adjust accordingly to minimize stress.

Touch and Environmental Awareness

Bearded dragons are sensitive to touch, especially around the face, tail, and limbs. While their spiny scales look rough, the skin underneath is quite delicate. Most dragons tolerate handling well once they trust you, but they prefer gentle, slow movements. Some even learn to enjoy being stroked along the back or behind the head.

They also sense temperature changes through their skin. Because they rely on external heat to regulate body temperature, they'll often move between warm and cool areas throughout the day. You may notice your dragon spreading its body out while basking to absorb more heat or lifting slightly when it feels too warm.

Conclusion: Seeing the World Through Their Senses

Your bearded dragon doesn't see, smell, or hear exactly as you do, but its senses are finely tuned to help it thrive. From spotting movement with laser-like focus to tasting the air with a flick of the tongue, every sense plays a role in how it interprets and navigates its environment.

By understanding these sensory systems, you can better meet your dragon's needs, interpret its behaviors, and deepen the bond between you. The more you observe how your dragon uses its senses, the more you'll realize just how intelligent and aware these ancient-looking reptiles truly are.

Chapter 10
Lifespan and Health Milestones

Bringing a bearded dragon into your life means making a long-term commitment. These reptiles may not live as long as cats or dogs, but with proper care, they can offer over a decade of calm companionship. Understanding their typical lifespan, what to expect at each life stage, and key health milestones can help you provide the best care possible—and recognize early signs of trouble before they become serious.

Typical Lifespan in Captivity

In the wild, bearded dragons often live 4 to 6 years due to predation, injury, and environmental stress. In captivity, however, where food is plentiful and threats are minimal, a healthy dragon can live between **8 to 12 years**. Some even reach 14 or more with excellent care.

Lifespan depends on several factors: genetics, diet, habitat quality, stress levels, lighting, and medical attention. Dragons from responsible breeders, raised with proper UVB lighting, balanced nutrition, and mental stimulation, tend to live longer, healthier lives.

Life Stage Milestones

1. **Hatchling (0–2 months):**

Tiny and fragile, hatchlings are entirely dependent on their environment. They need frequent feedings, high heat, and low-stress handling. This stage is marked by rapid growth and constant shedding.

2. **Juvenile (2–6 months):**

Your dragon will grow quickly during this period, possibly gaining several inches each month. Expect frequent shedding, a strong appetite (mostly for insects), and a burst of energy. Establishing a good calcium routine now is vital for bone health.

3. **Sub-Adult (6–12 months):**

Growth continues, though at a slower pace. Hormonal changes may lead to dominance displays, especially in males. Appetite may vary, and you'll start seeing adult behavior patterns emerge. By the end of this stage, your dragon is nearing full size.

4. **Adult (12 months–6 years):**

During adulthood, growth plateaus. Appetite stabilizes, activity levels may decrease slightly, and feeding needs shift toward more vegetables and less protein. This is a period of maintenance—keeping UVB lighting updated, offering enrichment, and watching for weight gain or mobility changes.

5. **Senior (6+ years):**

Older dragons slow down. You may notice less movement, occasional appetite dips, or reduced basking. Some develop arthritis or need softer food. Regular vet checkups are especially important in this stage to catch age-related issues early.

Key Health Milestones

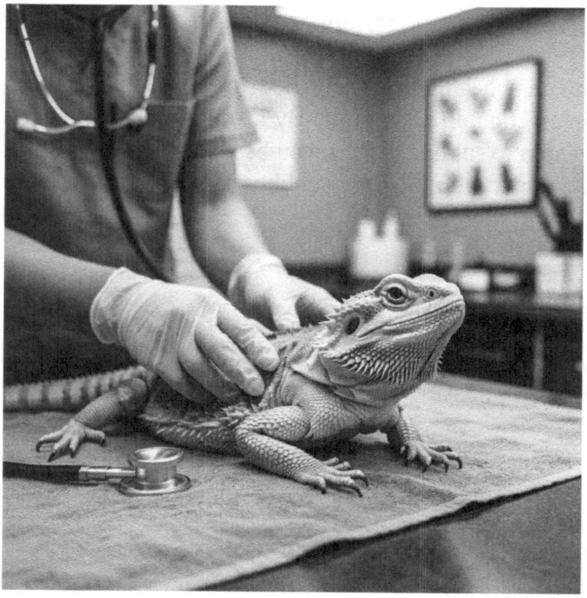

Regular Shedding:

Shedding is normal and occurs more often in young dragons. If your dragon has difficulty shedding, especially around the tail or toes, offer warm baths and increase humidity slightly.

- **Weight and Body Condition:**

A healthy adult should have a plump tail base, alert eyes, and a broad, firm body. Sudden weight loss or a sunken appearance can indicate illness, parasites, or poor nutrition.

- **Bowel Movements:**

Frequency varies depending on age and diet. Hatchlings may go daily; adults may go every few days. Long gaps, hard stools, or visible blood can signal impaction or other digestive issues.

- **Reproductive Milestones:**

Females may lay infertile eggs starting around 18 months. Provide a lay box and monitor calcium levels to prevent egg-binding. Males may display territorial or mating behaviors as early as 8–10 months.

- **Brumation:**

Many adult dragons slow down during cooler months in a hibernation-like state called brumation. Appetite drops, movement decreases, and they may sleep for days or weeks. This is normal, but it's wise to monitor hydration and check for underlying illness if behavior seems off.

Conclusion: Supporting a Long, Healthy Life

Your bearded dragon's health is closely tied to your daily choices—lighting, diet, cleanliness, and interaction all play a role. By learning the rhythms of their growth and aging, and staying alert to subtle changes, you become more than a keeper. You become a true companion on their journey from hatchling to wise, mellow elder.

Part 3
Behavior & Communication

Chapter 11
Common Behaviors – Understanding Your Bearded Dragon's Body Language

Bearded dragons may not speak, but they're far from silent. Through subtle and sometimes comical movements, they express everything from curiosity and contentment to fear and dominance. Observing and understanding these common behaviors is one of the most rewarding parts of owning a bearded dragon. It helps you build trust, identify emotional states, and even detect health or environmental issues early.

This chapter explores the most common bearded dragon behaviors, including head bobbing, arm waving, glass surfing, basking, color changes, and more—each with its possible meanings.

Head Bobbing

One of the most well-known and frequently observed behaviors, head bobbing is used for communication. Your dragon may quickly bob its head up and down in different ways, depending on the context.

- **Fast, assertive bobs** are typically a sign of dominance. Males do this most often to establish territory, intimidate rivals, or impress females. It can also occur if your dragon sees its reflection and mistakes it for another lizard.
- **Slower, more rhythmic bobbing** may be part of courtship, especially when accompanied by a blackened beard. It's often directed toward females or during breeding season behaviors.
- **Occasional bobbing toward humans** can happen too. It may mean your dragon is feeling territorial, curious, or unsure of your intentions—especially if you're entering its enclosure or handling it suddenly.

Head bobbing can look intense, but it's a natural and healthy form of expression.

Arm Waving

In contrast to the dominant head bob, arm waving is a submissive gesture. Your dragon will lift one front leg, rotate it in a slow circular motion, and then lower it again—almost like a little wave.

This behavior is most common in younger dragons and females, especially when housed near another dragon. It's a way of saying, "I see you, and I'm not a threat." In group settings, arm waving is often paired with a slower head bob from the submissive dragon, while the dominant one may respond with faster, firmer movements.

Sometimes, dragons will even wave at their reflections or at unfamiliar objects or people. It's a mix of curiosity and mild nervousness, and it usually stops once the dragon becomes familiar with its surroundings.

Basking and Flattening

Bearded dragons are cold-blooded and depend on heat from external sources. That's why you'll often find your dragon sprawled under its heat lamp, flattening its body to maximize surface area.

This flattened pose is called **"pancaking"** and helps them absorb more warmth quickly. You may also notice them darken in color during basking—darker scales absorb heat more efficiently. Once they're warm enough, they often lighten their color and move to a shaded spot.

Occasional mouth gaping during basking is normal too. This is a form of thermoregulation, helping them release excess heat, and is not a sign of aggression or illness unless accompanied by labored breathing or lethargy.

Color Changes

- Your bearded dragon's skin tone is more than just a fashion statement—it's a mood indicator. They can darken, lighten, or display specific color patches in response to temperature, emotions, or health.

- **Dark beard:** Often signals stress, fear, or dominance. It's commonly seen during introductions to new environments, rival dragons, or unfamiliar people.

- **Overall darkening:** Usually related to basking, helping absorb more heat.
- **Sudden lightness or dullness:** May indicate stress, brumation, or shedding. Some dragons appear grayer before they shed, which is completely normal.

Observing these color shifts over time helps you better understand your dragon's comfort level and routine.

Glass Surfing

If you've ever seen your dragon frantically scratching at the glass or standing on its hind legs while "paddling" its front legs, that's **glass surfing**. It often means your dragon is trying to escape or feels uncomfortable.

Possible reasons include:

- Enclosure is too small or lacks stimulation
- Lighting or temperature issues
- Seeing their reflection and mistaking it for another dragon
- Feeling anxious or bored

While this behavior isn't harmful in itself, prolonged glass surfing suggests something in the habitat may need adjusting. Try reviewing temperature gradients, hiding spots, and enrichment activities.

Digging and Burrowing

Bearded dragons naturally dig in the wild—to create burrows for sleep, regulate temperature, or lay eggs. In captivity, this behavior continues.

- **Female dragons** may dig more actively when gravid (carrying eggs), even if the eggs are infertile.
- **Both sexes** might dig when preparing for brumation or simply to create a comfy resting spot.

If your dragon is digging obsessively, consider providing a deeper, softer substrate in one part of the enclosure and ensure they have a proper hide.

Tail Twitching

Though less frequent, tail twitching can appear when your dragon is alert or preparing to pounce. You might see this behavior when they're hunting live insects or focused on something intriguing.

Mild tail movements are normal during hunting or exploring. However, if the tail is twitching uncontrollably or appears stiff or discolored, it could be a sign of nerve issues or injury and should be evaluated by a reptile vet.

Licking and Tongue Flicking

Dragons often flick their tongues at surfaces, objects, or people. This is how they gather chemical cues from their environment and interpret smells.

It's not a sign of hunger or aggression—it's simply how they explore. A dragon that flicks its tongue at you is usually showing interest, not hostility. It may also mean your dragon is getting used to your scent, especially in the early days of bonding.

Brumation Behavior

Brumation is a reptile's version of hibernation. During this period, often triggered by cooler seasons or changes in daylight, dragons become sluggish, sleep more, eat less, and may burrow into hides for days or weeks.

Not all dragons brumate, but when they do, it's important to support them:

- Keep the enclosure clean and slightly cooler
- Ensure hydration
- Avoid force-feeding

Brumation is a natural cycle and not a cause for alarm unless it occurs at an unusual age or with concerning symptoms like weight loss or lethargy outside the cool season.

Conclusion: Behavior as Communication

Your bearded dragon is always communicating, even without making a sound. Each head bob, arm wave, or glass scratch is a message. Learning to interpret these signals strengthens your connection with your pet and helps you respond in ways that support their comfort and health.

By observing, listening (in the visual sense), and responding with care, you become more than just a pet owner—you become a trusted part of your dragon's world. And over time, these small gestures build a bond that feels surprisingly deep, even between species.

Chapter 12
Body Language and Mood
How to Read Your Bearded Dragon

Bearded dragons are quiet creatures, but they have a rich vocabulary of movements and postures that reflect their emotions and needs. Once you learn how to interpret their body language, you'll unlock a deeper connection with your pet. Whether your dragon is content, anxious, dominant, or unwell, it uses its body to communicate. Understanding these signals allows you to respond appropriately and create a more comfortable, trusting environment for your companion.

This chapter helps you learn how to read your bearded dragon's mood through its posture, movements, color changes, and other visual cues.

Relaxed and Content Behavior

When your dragon is feeling safe, secure, and satisfied, its body language becomes easy to recognize.

- **Calm posture:** A relaxed dragon lies flat but not rigid, often stretched out with limbs loosely positioned. The tail rests gently behind the body.
- **Clear eyes:** Bright, alert eyes that follow movement without tension are signs of curiosity and ease.

- **Normal coloring:** The beard and body remain in their usual tones, with no darkening or puffing.
- **Tongue flicking:** A dragon that flicks its tongue lightly while exploring is simply investigating. This shows comfort and healthy curiosity.

You may also see your dragon basking quietly, shifting between warm and cool zones, or gently closing its eyes during a head rub—these are all signs of trust and contentment.

Alert and Curious

When something new catches your dragon's attention—a sound, object, or person—you'll likely notice a change in posture.

- **Raised body:** The dragon may lift itself slightly higher on its legs, giving it a more "perched" appearance.
- **Head tilt:** A tilted head, often combined with stillness, indicates focused curiosity. This is often seen when you approach the tank or present new food.
- **Tail curl:** A loosely curled tail, especially when basking or exploring, often shows excitement or anticipation.
- **Slow movements:** When cautious but interested, your dragon may move slowly toward the object of attention.

This body language reflects a healthy sense of awareness without stress. It's common in dragons that are well-socialized and comfortable in their space.

Stressed or Anxious

When your bearded dragon feels uneasy, overwhelmed, or unsafe, it expresses that discomfort through posture and behavior.

- **Dark beard:** One of the most visible signs of stress. The beard may darken dramatically, even if not puffed out. This often happens during relocation, loud noises, temperature issues, or new environments.
- **Hunched body:** A stressed dragon may crouch lower to the ground with tense limbs, eyes wide open, and movements that seem hesitant.
- **Glass surfing:** Frantic scratching at the enclosure walls often indicates restlessness or discomfort. Your dragon may be trying to escape or reacting to environmental problems.
- **Lack of appetite:** If paired with other signs of stress, refusing food can signal a deeper issue.

Stress may also show through excessive hiding, pacing, or changes in sleep habits. Regular observation helps you learn your dragon's baseline behavior so you can detect stress early.

Defensive and Threatened

In moments of fear or perceived threat, your dragon may adopt a defensive posture to protect itself or intimidate what it sees as danger.

- **Puffed beard and body:** To appear larger, your dragon may puff up its body and beard, sometimes hissing or opening its mouth slightly.
- **Rigid tail:** The tail becomes stiff and straight, often accompanied by tense limbs and flattened posture.
- **Bobbing head quickly:** Fast, jerky head bobs can be a warning to back off, especially if directed at a reflection, another dragon, or a person.
- **Turning sideways:** This posture maximizes body size, often used when confronting a perceived rival or threat.

If your dragon is reacting this way toward you, it's best to give space, lower your presence (sit or kneel), and let it calm down before attempting to interact again.

Submissive and Passive Behavior

Not all dragons are dominant. Some prefer a more passive or submissive role and show body language that reflects acceptance rather than confrontation.

- **Arm waving:** A slow, circular motion of the front leg often indicates submission or acknowledgment of another's dominance. It may also show uncertainty when exposed to new surroundings or dragons.
- **Flattened posture without puffing:** If your dragon lowers itself without appearing tense, it may be showing deference or trying to appear non-threatening.
- **Avoiding eye contact:** Looking away or keeping the body angled away can be a sign of nervousness or passive behavior.

Submissive dragons may take longer to warm up to handling and may benefit from more patience and gentle interaction.

Playful or Energetic Mood

While bearded dragons aren't playful in the way mammals are, they do exhibit lively and exploratory behavior when they're stimulated and content.

- **Climbing and exploring:** If your dragon is actively moving, climbing decor, or pacing with alert posture, it may simply be in an energetic mood.
- **Chasing insects or food:** This kind of focused hunting behavior, often paired with tail curling, indicates excitement and a natural burst of activity.
- **Tongue flicking while walking:** Suggests your dragon is comfortable enough to engage with its environment in a curious, playful way.

Enrichment through new objects, supervised outside-the-tank time, or variety in diet can encourage these healthy bursts of energy.

Sick or Lethargic Behavior

Unusual body language may also signal illness or injury. While these signs vary, some postures indicate it's time for a vet visit.

- **Limp limbs or tail:** Dragging body parts or weakness in the legs can signal metabolic issues or nerve problems.
- **Swollen body or jaws:** Visible swelling is always a red flag.
- **Eyes half-shut or sunken:** Tired or sunken eyes, especially when paired with lack of movement, may indicate dehydration or infection.
- **Unusual posture while sleeping or basking:** A dragon that no longer seeks heat, avoids basking entirely, or stays curled in a corner may be unwell.

Any dramatic or persistent change in posture or mood should be taken seriously, especially if paired with changes in appetite, bowel habits, or coloration.

Conclusion: Reading the Silent Language

Your bearded dragon may never utter a sound, but it's constantly telling you how it feels. Through posture, color, movement, and small gestures, it communicates stress, interest, comfort, fear, or calm. Learning this body language helps you become a more attentive and compassionate caretaker.

By slowing down, observing closely, and responding appropriately, you create a relationship built on trust. And in that silent, visual language, your dragon learns that you're not just the one who brings food or adjusts the lights—you're someone who listens.

Chapter 13
Social Hierarchies

Bearded dragons are generally solitary creatures in the wild, but when kept in captivity—especially in shared enclosures or breeding situations—they establish clear social hierarchies. These hierarchies determine dominance, territory, and access to basking spots or food. Understanding how these pecking orders work is essential if you're housing more than one dragon or observing them interact.

Dominance is usually asserted through body language. The most dominant dragon will often occupy the highest perch in the enclosure and may perform frequent, rapid head bobs. It may also puff its beard, darken in color, and stand tall to appear larger. Subordinate dragons will typically respond by waving their arms slowly in a circle or lowering their bodies in submission.

Physical aggression is rare when dragons have enough space and can communicate effectively, but in cramped or overstimulating environments, fights can break out. Biting, chasing, and tail nipping are serious signs of conflict and should not be ignored.

It's generally not recommended to house adult bearded dragons together, especially males. Two males will almost always challenge each other for dominance, leading to stress and injury. Even housing a male and female together long-term can be problematic, as the male may relentlessly pursue mating, causing the female stress or exhaustion.

Juveniles may be more tolerant of shared space for short periods, but as they mature, the drive to establish dominance becomes stronger. If you must house multiple dragons, always provide ample space, multiple basking and feeding zones, and monitor behavior closely.

Social hierarchy is a natural part of bearded dragon behavior, but in captivity, it can lead to chronic stress for the submissive dragon. If one dragon consistently loses weight, hides, or becomes lethargic, it may be time to separate them. Paying attention to these dynamics helps ensure all dragons stay healthy and stress-free.

Chapter 14
Mating Behavior

Mating behavior in bearded dragons is driven by seasonal and hormonal cues, typically triggered by changes in daylight, temperature, or brumation cycles. When these cues align—often in spring—both male and female dragons begin to display distinct reproductive behaviors.

Males become more territorial and assertive. You'll notice strong, fast head bobs, blackened beards, and heightened activity. They may also circle the female, stomp their front legs, and perform repeated head jerks. This display is meant to assert dominance and attract a mate.

Females, in contrast, may display submissive arm waving or crouching. If receptive, the female usually remains still, allowing the male to mount. Mating itself is brief but can be rough. The male typically bites the female's neck or shoulder to hold her in place—a normal, though sometimes alarming, behavior to observe.

After successful mating, the female may become visibly round or swollen in the abdomen within a few weeks. Gravid females (those carrying eggs) will often dig or scratch as they search for a suitable nesting area. Providing a lay box with moist substrate is crucial during this time to help her lay eggs safely.

Mating should always be carefully supervised. Overbreeding or housing males and females together long-term can lead to exhaustion, injury, and stress—especially for the female. Once mating is complete, it's best to separate the pair.

If you plan to breed dragons, ensure both are healthy, mature (at least 18 months old), and from different bloodlines to avoid genetic issues. Responsible breeding includes proper incubation, preparation for egg-laying, and care for hatchlings. Without the right planning and conditions, breeding can do more harm than good.

By recognizing and respecting these natural behaviors, you can create a safe and healthy environment during the mating process—whether your goal is breeding or simply understanding your dragon's seasonal changes.

Chapter 15
Brumation (Reptile Hibernation)

Brumation is a natural, hibernation-like state that many reptiles—including bearded dragons—enter during colder months. It's a seasonal slowdown, triggered by reduced daylight, cooler temperatures, and instinct. While it can be alarming the first time you see it, brumation is a normal part of a healthy bearded dragon's life cycle.

During brumation, your dragon's metabolism slows dramatically. It may sleep for long periods, eat very little or nothing at all, and spend most of its time hiding in a cool, dark spot. In the wild, this behavior helps conserve energy when food and warmth are scarce. Even in captivity, where conditions are controlled, many dragons still follow this natural rhythm.

Not all dragons brumate. Younger dragons under 10 months old typically don't, and some adults may skip it entirely depending on their environment or genetics. If your dragon begins showing signs—like refusing food, digging, sleeping more, or spending time in cooler areas—it may be preparing for brumation.

You should never force brumation. If your dragon chooses to go into this state, reduce the basking temperature slightly (to around 85°F), provide a quiet hide, and stop offering food once it's clear your dragon is no longer eating. Forcing food during this time can lead to digestive issues since their system is too slow to process it properly.

Hydration remains important. Even during brumation, offer brief, warm soaks every few weeks to ensure your dragon doesn't become dehydrated. You don't need to turn off UVB or basking lights completely but can reduce their duration to mimic shorter days.

A brumation period may last anywhere from a few weeks to three months. When your dragon becomes active again, resume normal lighting, basking, and feeding routines. Appetite usually returns gradually, so offer small meals at first and monitor behavior.

If your dragon loses significant weight, seems unusually lethargic, or exhibits any signs of illness, consult a reptile vet before assuming it's brumation. Clear eyes, healthy skin, and calm behavior usually mean your dragon is just resting.

Brumation is a fascinating survival instinct and not a cause for worry when understood. By supporting your dragon through it safely, you respect its natural rhythms—and provide care that goes beyond the surface.

Part 4
Habitat Setup & Environment

Chapter 16
Ideal Enclosure Size

A bearded dragon's enclosure isn't just a box—it's their entire world. From basking to sleeping, climbing to digging, your dragon relies on its habitat for every aspect of its physical and mental well-being. One of the most important—and often overlooked—parts of proper setup is ensuring the enclosure is the right size.

A cramped or undersized enclosure can lead to stress, limited movement, aggression, improper thermoregulation, and even long-term health problems. On the other hand, a spacious, well-organized enclosure allows your dragon to move freely, express natural behaviors, and feel secure.

Minimum Size Guidelines by Age

1. Hatchlings (0–2 months)

For very young dragons under 6 inches long, a **20-gallon tank** (24" x 12" x 16") is sufficient for the first few weeks. This smaller space helps them find food easily and reduces stress.

2. Juveniles (2–6 months)

Once your dragon reaches about 10 inches, it will need much more room to move and grow. A **40-gallon breeder tank** (36" x 18" x 18") is a common next step. This size supports active climbing, exploring, and proper heat zoning.

3. Sub-Adults and Adults (6 months and older)

Adult bearded dragons require a **minimum of 75 gallons** (48" x 18" x 21"). However, **120 gallons or larger** is ideal. Enclosures that are at least **4 feet long, 2 feet wide, and 2 feet tall** offer the best quality of life. Larger dragons, especially males over 20 inches, benefit from even more space.

Why Bigger Is Better

Bearded dragons are ground-dwelling but semi-arboreal—they enjoy climbing, digging, and moving between hot and cool zones. In a spacious enclosure, you can provide proper basking and hiding spots, climbing branches, feeding dishes, and room to roam.

Larger enclosures also make it easier to establish the correct **temperature gradient**, with a hot side for basking and a cooler side for resting. Without enough room, it's hard to maintain this gradient, which can impact digestion and thermoregulation.

Additionally, extra space reduces stress, encourages exercise, and allows for more natural behavior. This is especially helpful for mental enrichment, which is vital for long-term well-being.

What to Avoid

Avoid vertical tanks or enclosures that are tall but not wide. Bearded dragons need horizontal space to move and regulate their body temperature, not just height. Also, never house two adult dragons together in one enclosure, no matter the size—territorial stress can lead to injury or death.

Conclusion

The size of your bearded dragon's enclosure directly affects its quality of life. While smaller tanks may work temporarily for babies, always plan for growth. Investing in a spacious, well-designed habitat from the start ensures your dragon has the freedom to thrive—not just survive.

Chapter 17
Substrates – Safe and Unsafe Options

Substrate refers to the material that lines the bottom of your bearded dragon's enclosure. It may seem like a minor detail, but the type of substrate you choose can significantly affect your dragon's health, hygiene, and comfort. The wrong substrate can lead to serious problems like impaction (a life-threatening digestive blockage), respiratory issues, or even bacterial infections. Choosing the right substrate means creating a safe, natural-feeling environment that supports your dragon's lifestyle while minimizing risk.

Let's break down the safest options first—then cover what to avoid.

Safe Substrate Options

1. Reptile Carpet

This is one of the most popular and widely recommended substrates for beginners. Made from soft, washable fabric, reptile carpet is reusable, easy to clean, and safe for all ages.

- **Pros:** Non-loose, no risk of impaction, available in most pet stores
- **Cons:** Can trap odor if not cleaned regularly; claws may occasionally snag on fibers

Make sure to keep two carpets and rotate them—wash one while using the other.

2. Tile (Ceramic or Slate)

Tiles offer a sleek, hygienic option that's both attractive and functional. They retain heat well, aiding in thermoregulation.

- **Pros:** Durable, easy to clean, zero impaction risk, helps keep claws filed
- **Cons:** Can be slippery if wet; requires proper fitting to avoid sharp edges or shifting

Many keepers use textured tiles to give better grip.

3. Paper Towels or Newspaper

Ideal for hatchlings, sick dragons, or temporary quarantine setups, paper substrates are cheap and easy to replace.

- **Pros:** Inexpensive, hygienic, no risk of impaction
- **Cons:** Not visually appealing, needs frequent changing, offers no enrichment

4. Rubber Shelf Liner or Non-Adhesive Mats

Soft and easy to clean, these materials can provide a cushiony feel underfoot while remaining low-risk.

- **Pros:** Affordable, customizable, easy to wipe down
- **Cons:** Can retain odors or stain over time

Unsafe Substrate Options

1. **Loose Sand (Calcium or Play Sand)**

Though commonly marketed for desert reptiles, loose sand—especially calcium-based sand—is one of the most dangerous substrates. If ingested, it can compact in the digestive system, leading to impaction. Even careful feeding won't prevent accidental ingestion, especially in curious or young dragons.

- **Risk:** High impaction risk, dust inhalation, bacterial growth

2. **Wood Chips, Bark, or Mulch**

These substrates are too coarse and splintery for bearded dragons. Sharp edges can injure the mouth, and ingestion is a real concern. Some types also hold humidity, which can create respiratory problems.

- **Risk:** Impaction, injury, mold, and splinters

3. **Gravel, Pebbles, or Crushed Walnut**

These may look decorative, but they are among the most dangerous options. They're indigestible, can't be passed if swallowed, and offer no comfort or enrichment.

- **Risk:** Severe impaction, hard on feet and claws

4. **Soil or Dirt (Unsterilized)**

While some experienced keepers use bioactive setups with soil, these require precise control of moisture, microbial balance, and cleaning. Unsterilized soil can harbor parasites and bacteria.

- **Risk:** Parasites, mold, inconsistent humidity

Conclusion

Substrate isn't just a background detail—it's part of your dragon's everyday life. Choosing a safe, clean, and comfortable option helps prevent health issues and makes enclosure maintenance easier. While naturalistic environments can be tempting, your dragon's safety should always come first. Stick with tried-and-tested substrates like tile, reptile carpet, or paper products to ensure a happy, healthy life for your bearded buddy.

Chapter 18
Lighting & UVB Needs

Bearded dragons are sun-loving reptiles, native to the open, sun-drenched environments of Australia. In the wild, they rely on natural sunlight not only for warmth but also for essential biological functions. In captivity, where sunlight isn't available, it's your responsibility to replicate those lighting conditions as closely as possible. Proper lighting is not just about visibility—it's vital for your dragon's bone health, appetite, mood, and overall survival.

Let's explore the types of lighting your bearded dragon needs, with a special focus on UVB, and how to set up a lighting system that supports a long and healthy life.

Why Lighting Matters

Bearded dragons are ectothermic (cold-blooded), which means they depend on external heat sources to regulate their body temperature. Without proper heating and lighting, they can't digest food, fight infection, or maintain energy levels. Just as importantly, they need **ultraviolet B (UVB)** light to produce vitamin D3, which allows their bodies to absorb calcium from food.

Without UVB, even a calcium-rich diet becomes useless, eventually leading to **metabolic bone disease (MBD)**—a painful, debilitating, and often irreversible condition. This is why lighting setup is not optional; it's a foundational part of care.

Types of Lighting Your Dragon Needs

1. Basking Light (Heat Source)

Your dragon needs a bright, warm spot in the tank to raise its body temperature during the day.

- **Purpose:** Thermoregulation and digestion
- **Placement:** One end of the enclosure to create a heat gradient
- **Ideal Basking Temperature:**
  - Hatchlings: 105–110°F
  - Juveniles and Adults: 100–105°F
  - Cool side of tank: 75–85°F

Use a dome-style heat bulb with a ceramic fixture to safely direct heat downward. Monitor temperature with a digital probe thermometer placed at the basking site.

2. UVB Light (Full-Spectrum Fluorescent)

UVB is essential for synthesizing vitamin D3. There are two main types of UVB bulbs:

- **Tube-style (T5 or T8):** Preferred for reliability and coverage. T5 high-output bulbs are ideal and should be mounted 10–18 inches above the basking spot.
- **Compact bulbs:** Less effective due to narrow beam and inconsistent output. Use only if space is limited and UVB output is confirmed with a meter.

Replace UVB bulbs every **6 to 12 months**, even if they still emit light—UVB output fades over time.

Lighting Schedule

Bearded dragons follow a day-night rhythm. Your lighting setup should mimic natural daylight hours.

- **Daytime:** 12–14 hours of full lighting (basking and UVB)
- **Nighttime:** Complete darkness. No light is needed, and colored bulbs can disrupt sleep cycles.

Use a timer to keep lighting consistent. This helps regulate brumation, appetite, and overall mood.

Tips for a Proper Setup

- Mount the UVB bulb **inside the enclosure** if the tank has a mesh top—mesh filters out some UVB rays.
- Avoid placing clear plastic or glass between your dragon and the UVB source, as it blocks UVB.
- Position the basking bulb and UVB light on the **same side** of the enclosure. This way, your dragon receives both heat and UVB while basking.

Conclusion

Proper lighting is more than a checklist item—it's the key to your bearded dragon's health. Without UVB and a suitable heat source, even the best diet won't be enough. Invest in high-quality bulbs, maintain the right temperatures and light cycles, and replace bulbs as needed. With the right setup, you're not just providing light—you're replicating the sun and everything it brings to your dragon's world.

Chapter 19
Temperature and Humidity Zones

Bearded dragons come from the dry, sunbaked regions of Australia, where they've adapted to wide temperature swings and low humidity. To thrive in captivity, they need a carefully maintained environment that mimics these conditions—especially when it comes to **temperature gradients** and **humidity levels**.

Unlike mammals, bearded dragons regulate their body temperature by moving between warm and cool areas. This is why your enclosure must have **clearly defined zones** that allow your dragon to choose how warm or cool it wants to be at any given time.

Temperature Zones

Your enclosure should have three main temperature areas:

1. **Basking Zone (Hot Side):**

This is the warmest part of the tank, where your dragon can heat up after sleeping or eating.

- Hatchlings: 105–110°F
- Juveniles: 100–105°F
- Adults: 95–100°F

Place a heat bulb directly over a basking platform like a rock or tile. Use a digital probe thermometer to check temperature right at the surface.

2. **Cool Side:**

On the opposite end of the tank, the cool zone allows your dragon to retreat when it's too warm.

- Ideal range: 75–85°F during the day
- At night: 65–75°F is acceptable and mimics natural temperature drops

3. **Ambient (Middle Zone):**

The middle part of the tank should offer a balanced temperature between the hot and cool sides—generally 85–90°F.

This temperature gradient helps with digestion, immune function, and comfort. Without it, your dragon may become stressed, lethargic, or unable to regulate its body properly.

Humidity Zones

Bearded dragons need a **dry environment** to stay healthy. High humidity can lead to respiratory infections, mold growth, and skin issues.

- **Ideal Humidity Level:** 30–40%
- Use a hygrometer to measure humidity in the enclosure, especially near the basking and cool zones. Avoid misting the tank unless shedding requires extra humidity. A shallow water bowl placed on the cool side may help maintain safe levels without raising moisture too much.

Conclusion

Creating the right temperature and humidity zones is essential for your bearded dragon's health. With a well-balanced gradient, your dragon can self-regulate, stay active, and feel at home—just like it would in the Australian outback.

Chapter 20
Hides, Climbing Areas, and Enrichment

Bearded dragons are intelligent, observant, and instinct-driven reptiles. While warmth, lighting, and food keep them alive, environmental enrichment keeps them mentally and physically healthy. In the wild, they explore diverse terrain, bask on rocks, hide in crevices, and dig shallow burrows. Recreating this dynamic environment in captivity is not only possible—it's essential for your dragon's long-term well-being.

In this chapter, you'll learn how to set up hides, climbing areas, and enrichment features that stimulate your dragon's natural instincts while creating a more comfortable and engaging habitat.

Hides: Safe Spaces to Rest and Retreat

Every bearded dragon enclosure should include at least one hide box, preferably two—one on the **cool side** and another on the **warm side** of the tank. Hides provide your dragon with a sense of safety, a place to sleep, cool down, or de-stress.

Why hides matter:

- Offer security from overstimulation or stress
- Help regulate temperature by giving choices
- Provide privacy during shedding or brumation
- Reduce anxiety in new environments

Hides can be simple (a wooden half-log or commercial reptile cave) or custom (rock-like resin structures or DIY shelters made from non-toxic materials). Ensure the hide is large enough for your dragon to turn around comfortably but still snug enough to feel secure.

Climbing Areas: Encourage Activity and Basking

Bearded dragons are not strictly ground-dwelling—they love to climb. In the wild, they perch on logs, rocks, and low branches to survey their territory or bask in the sun. Adding vertical elements to your enclosure helps replicate this natural behavior and prevents boredom.

Popular climbing features include:

- Branches (real or synthetic, sanitized)
- Stacked slate or flat rocks
- Hammocks or platforms
- Reptile-safe climbing shelves

Place climbing structures near the **basking zone** to allow your dragon to choose its optimal height and warmth. Always ensure climbing items are secure, stable, and do not shift under weight. This prevents injury and encourages daily movement.

Enrichment: Mental and Physical Stimulation

Enrichment is any activity or object that encourages natural behavior. Without stimulation, bearded dragons can become bored, lethargic, or even stressed. Enrichment doesn't have to be complicated—it just needs to engage the senses and promote curiosity.

Effective enrichment ideas:

- **Exploration time outside the tank:** Allow your dragon to explore a safe, enclosed area under supervision. A dragon-safe room or playpen gives them new surfaces, scents, and sights.
- **Rearranging decor:** Occasionally changing the layout inside the tank introduces novelty without overwhelming them.
- **Live feeders:** Watching and hunting live insects (like crickets or dubia roaches) provides both exercise and engagement.
- **Food puzzles:** Offer leafy greens in a small hanging basket or place veggies inside a wiffle ball to encourage foraging.
- **Textures and tunnels:** Introduce safe materials like cork bark, fabric tunnels, or textured stones for tactile stimulation.

You can even place your dragon near a sunny window (without glass between them and UVB light) or let them watch you from a safe perch. Bearded dragons enjoy visual activity and may respond to moving shapes, light, or your presence.

Conclusion

A thoughtfully arranged enclosure with hides, climbing options, and enrichment activities transforms your dragon's tank from a basic habitat into a stimulating and comfortable home. These additions mimic natural behaviors, reduce stress, and keep your dragon both physically active and mentally alert. With just a bit of creativity and observation, you can create an environment that your dragon will love exploring every day.

Part 5
Diet & Nutrition

Chapter 21
What Do They Eat?
(Insects, Greens, Veggies)

Bearded dragons are omnivores, which means they eat a mix of both plant and animal matter. In the wild, they consume a diverse diet that includes insects, leafy greens, flowers, and the occasional fruit. Replicating this varied and balanced diet in captivity is one of the most important parts of caring for your dragon. Not only does it keep them physically healthy, but it also stimulates natural hunting and foraging behaviors that contribute to their overall well-being.

In this chapter, you'll learn about the different types of food bearded dragons eat—including insects, vegetables, greens, and treats—as well as how to build a healthy diet at every life stage.

Insects: Protein-Packed Essentials

Insects are a major component of a young bearded dragon's diet. They provide protein for muscle growth, fat for energy, and stimulation through the hunt. However, not all insects are equally nutritious.

Best feeder insects:

- **Crickets:** A classic staple—easy to find, affordable, and accepted by most dragons. They should be gut-loaded (fed nutritious food before being served) and dusted with calcium.
- **Dubia roaches:** Higher in protein and easier to digest than crickets. They're quieter, cleaner, and less likely to escape.
- **Black soldier fly larvae (Phoenix worms):** High in calcium, making them an excellent daily feeder.
- **Silkworms and hornworms:** Hydrating and nutritious, but best used as occasional feeders due to cost and availability.
- Insects to avoid:
- **Mealworms and superworms:** High in fat and difficult to digest because of their hard exoskeletons. Can be given sparingly to adults.
- **Wild-caught bugs:** These may carry pesticides, parasites, or bacteria that can harm your dragon.
- **Fireflies and lightning bugs:** Highly toxic—even a small amount can be fatal.

Feeding guidelines:

- **Hatchlings and juveniles (0–6 months):** 70–80% of their diet should be protein from insects.

- **Sub-adults and adults (6 months+):** Gradually reduce insects to 30–40% of the diet, increasing plant-based foods as they mature.

Feed live insects in short, timed feeding sessions (10–15 minutes) and remove any uneaten insects afterward.

Leafy Greens: The Daily Staple

As bearded dragons grow, greens become the cornerstone of their diet. These provide fiber, hydration, vitamins, and minerals.

Best greens (feed daily):

- Collard greens
- Mustard greens
- Dandelion greens
- Turnip greens
- Endive
- Escarole

These greens are rich in calcium and low in oxalates, making them excellent staples. Wash thoroughly and chop them into small pieces for easy eating.

Greens to offer occasionally:

- Kale (high in oxalates but fine in moderation)
- Bok choy
- Spinach (only in very small amounts due to calcium-binding properties)

Greens to avoid:

- Iceberg lettuce (nutritionally empty and mostly water)
- Swiss chard and beet greens (high in oxalates)

Offer greens daily, even to young dragons—even if they mostly ignore them at first. With consistency, they'll develop healthy eating habits over time.

Vegetables: Variety and Nutrition

Chopped vegetables add color, texture, and variety to your dragon's meals. They also supply additional nutrients and water content.

Great vegetables:

- Bell peppers (any color, raw)
- Squash (butternut, acorn, yellow—shredded or thinly sliced)
- Carrots (in moderation)
- Zucchini
- Cucumber (hydrating, but low in nutrients)

Vegetables to use sparingly:

- Tomatoes (acidic and best offered as a treat)
- Broccoli (high in goitrogens; offer rarely)

Unsafe vegetables:

- Avocado (toxic to reptiles)
- Onion and garlic (irritating and harmful)

Mix vegetables into the salad base with greens and rotate selections often to avoid boredom.

Fruits and Treats

Fruits should be fed sparingly, mainly as treats. Too much sugar can disrupt digestion and contribute to obesity.

Safe fruits (once or twice a week):

- Blueberries
- Strawberries
- Papaya
- Mango
- Apples (peeled and seeded)
- Watermelon (hydrating, but low in nutrients)

Chop fruit into small pieces and mix with veggies to encourage interest, especially for picky eaters.

Calcium and Vitamin Supplements

Even with a balanced diet, captive bearded dragons need **calcium and vitamin supplementation** to prevent deficiencies.

- **Calcium powder (without D3):** Dust insects 4–5 times per week.
- **Multivitamin powder:** Use 1–2 times per week.
- **Calcium with D3:** Use only if your dragon is not getting UVB exposure. Otherwise, D3 should come from UVB lighting.

Too much supplementation can be harmful, so stick to a consistent schedule based on age and lighting conditions.

Hydration and Water

Though dragons get much of their moisture from food, they still need access to clean, shallow drinking water. Change it daily and keep the bowl on the cool side of the tank to avoid excessive humidity.

Some dragons prefer to drink while being misted or bathed. Offer a warm bath once or twice a week, which can also help during shedding.

Conclusion

A bearded dragon's diet is about more than just filling its belly—it's the foundation of health, growth, and longevity. By offering a balanced mix of protein-rich insects, calcium-dense greens, colorful vegetables, and the occasional fruit treat, you give your dragon the variety and nutrition it needs to thrive. With consistent feeding routines and mindful choices, mealtime becomes not just a necessity, but a highlight of your dragon's day.

Chapter 22
Feeding Schedule by Age

Bearded dragons have different dietary needs depending on their age, size, and activity level. A baby dragon growing at a rapid pace needs frequent, protein-rich meals. In contrast, an adult dragon thrives on a more plant-focused, controlled diet to maintain weight and long-term health.

Creating a feeding schedule that aligns with your dragon's developmental stage ensures proper growth, energy, bone strength, and digestion. In this chapter, you'll learn how often to feed, what to feed, and how to shift your dragon's diet as it matures—from a tiny hatchling to a laid-back adult.

Hatchlings (0–2 months)

Hatchlings are tiny and growing fast. At this stage, their diet should be heavily protein-focused with multiple feedings throughout the day.

- **Insects:** 3–5 times per day, offered in short sessions of 10–15 minutes
- **Greens:** Offered fresh daily, even if ignored
- **Calcium:** Dust insects with calcium 5 days per week
- **Multivitamin:** 1–2 times per week

Hatchlings may eat 30–80 small feeder insects (like pinhead crickets or tiny roaches) per day. Gut-load all insects before feeding. Don't leave uneaten feeders in the tank, as they can stress or bite the baby.

Juveniles (2–6 months)

This is still a high-growth stage, but the dragon begins exploring plant-based foods more regularly. You'll continue offering insects daily, but begin reducing the number of feedings.

- **Insects:** 2–3 times per day
- **Greens/Veggies:** Fresh daily
- **Calcium:** 5 times per week
- **Multivitamin:** 1–2 times per week

Introduce vegetables gradually. Dragons this age may begin showing preferences for certain greens, so keep rotating options.

Sub-Adults (6–12 months)

Growth begins to slow, and the need for protein decreases. The diet now starts shifting to include more greens and fewer insects.

- **Insects:** Once daily or every other day
- **Greens/Veggies:** Daily, now forming at least half the diet
- **Calcium:** 4–5 times per week
- **Multivitamin:** Once per week

During this stage, some dragons may seem picky or go through mini "brumation-like" slowdowns. Keep track of weight and hydration if appetite dips.

Adults (12 months and up)

Fully grown dragons need far less protein and should primarily eat plant matter. Overfeeding insects can lead to obesity and liver strain in adults.

- **Insects:** 2–3 times per week
- **Greens/Veggies:** Daily (70–80% of total diet)
- **Calcium:** 3–4 times per week
- **Multivitamin:** Once per week

Adult dragons often eat once per day or every other day. Feeding schedules can be flexible based on appetite, health, and season (e.g., during brumation, they may eat very little or nothing for weeks).

Feeding Table by Age

Age	Feeding Frequency	Insects	Greens/ Veggies	Calcium	Multivitamin
0–2 months	3–5 times daily	Tiny crickets, roaches, BSFL	Daily (even if ignored)	5 times per week	1–2 times per week
2–6 months	2–3 times daily	Small/ medium insects	Daily	5 times per week	1–2 times per week
6–12 months	Once daily or every other day	Medium/large insects	Daily	4–5 times per week	Once per week
12+ months	Once daily or every other day	2–3 times per week (as treats/ supplement)	Daily (main food source)	3–4 times per week	Once per week

Conclusion

Matching your dragon's feeding schedule to its age ensures healthy development in youth and disease prevention in adulthood. By offering the right food at the right time and adjusting as your dragon matures, you support a long, balanced, and active life. Remember: consistency, variety, and observation are the pillars of proper nutrition.

Chapter 23: Foods to Avoid

While bearded dragons enjoy a wide variety of foods, not everything that's safe for humans or other pets is safe for them. Some items can cause digestive issues, nutritional imbalances, or even toxic reactions. Knowing what **not** to feed is just as important as knowing what to offer.

Toxic Foods

These should never be given under any circumstances:

- **Avocado:** Contains persin, a toxin that is harmful and potentially fatal to reptiles.
- **Rhubarb:** Highly toxic; even small amounts can lead to organ failure.
- **Fireflies or lightning bugs:** Deadly to bearded dragons due to toxic chemicals in their bodies.
- **Onions and garlic:** Can irritate the digestive system and damage red blood cells.
- **Wild-caught insects:** May carry pesticides, parasites, or bacteria. Always use captive-bred feeders.

Foods High in Oxalates or Goitrogens

These block calcium absorption and interfere with thyroid function if fed too often:

- **Spinach**
- **Beet greens**
- **Swiss chard**
- **Cabbage**
- **Kale** (safe in moderation)
- Offer these rarely, and balance them with high-calcium greens.

Poor Nutritional Value or Risky Choices

- **Iceberg lettuce:** Mostly water, no real nutrients.
- **Citrus fruits (oranges, lemons):** Too acidic, may irritate the digestive tract.
- **Processed foods:** Anything salted, sweetened, or cooked—chips, bread, pasta, dairy—is unsuitable.
- **Meat and eggs:** Too high in fat and protein for a reptile's system. Stick with feeder insects.

Conclusion

Feeding your dragon the wrong items, even occasionally, can lead to serious health issues. When in doubt, stick to the basics: safe greens, vegetables, and approved insects. Always research new foods before offering them. A cautious diet is a safe diet.

Chapter 24
Hydration and Water Needs

Bearded dragons are native to the dry, arid regions of Australia where water sources are scarce. Because of this, they've evolved to be highly efficient at conserving moisture. However, in captivity, maintaining proper hydration is still essential for their health. Dehydration can lead to digestive issues, impaction, shedding problems, and kidney stress. The key is to offer hydration in ways that mimic how they would naturally obtain it—through food, occasional drinking, and environmental exposure.

How Bearded Dragons Stay Hydrated

In the wild, bearded dragons get most of their water from the insects and plants they eat, as well as from dew or rain droplets collected on surfaces. They rarely drink from standing water sources.

In captivity, you should continue this hydration strategy by:

- Offering water-rich vegetables like cucumber, squash, and bell peppers
- Providing a clean, shallow water dish
- Using occasional misting or bathing to encourage drinking and aid shedding

Water Bowl Basics

Even if your dragon doesn't drink from a bowl often, it's a good idea to keep one in the enclosure on the **cool side** to prevent excess evaporation. Use a shallow dish that's easy to access but not so deep that your dragon might struggle to climb out.

Change the water **daily**, and clean the bowl regularly to avoid bacterial buildup. Some dragons may defecate in their water dish, so regular checks are important.

Bathing for Hydration

Weekly warm baths serve two purposes: hydration and hygiene. Some dragons will lap at the water or absorb small amounts through their vent (cloaca). A warm soak (5–10 minutes) can also soften old skin during shedding and help stimulate bowel movements.

Always supervise bath time and make sure the water is shallow—no deeper than the dragon's elbows—and warm (not hot).

Misting and Droplets

Occasional light misting can encourage drinking, especially in younger dragons. Try misting the dragon's snout or dripping water onto their nose—many will lick it up. However, avoid misting too frequently, as excess humidity can lead to respiratory problems.

Signs of Dehydration

Watch for these symptoms:

- Wrinkled or saggy skin
- Sunken eyes
- Lethargy
- Lack of appetite
- Hard, dry stool

If you suspect dehydration, increase hydration efforts through bath soaks, water-rich veggies, and gentle misting. Persistent signs should be evaluated by a reptile veterinarian.

Conclusion

Bearded dragons don't need a lot of water—but they do need **enough** and in the **right forms**. By combining proper food choices with occasional soaking and accessible clean water, you'll ensure your dragon stays healthy, hydrated, and comfortable in its desert-inspired habitat.

Part 6
Care & Handling

Chapter 25
Calcium and Supplementation

Calcium is one of the most important nutrients in your bearded dragon's diet. Without it, their bones can become weak and deformed, muscles may cramp or twitch, and serious conditions like **metabolic bone disease (MBD)** can develop. In the wild, bearded dragons naturally obtain calcium through varied diets and sunlight exposure. In captivity, it's your job to make sure they get enough calcium and related supplements to support strong bones, healthy growth, and proper organ function.

Why Calcium Matters

Calcium is essential for:

- Bone and teeth strength
- Muscle contraction
- Nerve function
- Egg production in females

Without enough calcium—or the right balance of calcium and phosphorus—your dragon's body may begin pulling calcium from its bones, leading to brittle limbs, curved spines, jaw deformities, and even seizures.

The Role of Vitamin D3

Calcium cannot be absorbed properly without **vitamin D3**, which your dragon synthesizes through **UVB light exposure**. If a dragon doesn't get enough UVB, even a calcium-rich diet won't prevent deficiencies.

- If your dragon has access to **strong, high-quality UVB lighting**, use **calcium powder without D3** for daily supplementation.
- If UVB is limited or not working correctly, use **calcium with D3**, but not daily—too much D3 can be toxic.

UVB lighting should always be the primary source of D3 unless a vet recommends otherwise.

Supplement Types and Use

1. **Calcium Powder (with or without D3):**

   - Dust feeder insects **4–5 times per week** for juveniles
   - For adults, dust **3–4 times per week**
   - Lightly coat insects—don't oversaturate

2. **Multivitamin Powder:**

- Use **once per week** to provide additional vitamins like A, E, and B-complex
- Overuse can cause vitamin imbalances, so keep it occasional

Use a shaker or plastic bag to coat feeders evenly, and always supplement freshly gut-loaded insects for maximum nutrition.

Special Considerations for Females and Hatchlings

Gravid (egg-carrying) females require **extra calcium**, as eggshell formation pulls heavily on the body's reserves. Supplement daily and monitor closely for signs of fatigue or twitching.

Hatchlings and juveniles in rapid growth stages also need consistent calcium. Poor supplementation during this time can lead to irreversible skeletal deformities.

Conclusion

Calcium and supplements are silent protectors in your bearded dragon's life. You may not see their effects daily, but they play a critical role in preventing some of the most common and preventable health issues in captivity. With a proper balance of calcium, D3, multivitamins, and good lighting, you set your dragon up for a lifetime of strong bones, smooth shedding, and steady health.

Chapter 26
Daily, Weekly, Monthly Care Tasks

Caring for a bearded dragon involves more than feeding and switching on a light. These reptiles depend on a consistent and well-maintained environment to stay healthy and happy. A structured care routine helps prevent illness, ensures cleanliness, and keeps your dragon physically and mentally stimulated. Breaking down your responsibilities into daily, weekly, and monthly tasks makes care manageable and keeps your dragon's habitat in optimal condition.

Let's look at what you should do regularly to support your bearded dragon's well-being.

Daily Care Tasks

1. **Feeding:**

Offer fresh food—greens, vegetables, and insects based on age. Remove uneaten food within a few hours to avoid spoilage or pest attraction.

2. **Water Bowl Check:**

Clean and refill the water dish with fresh, dechlorinated water.

3. **Spot Cleaning:**

Remove feces, uneaten food, and shed skin to keep the enclosure clean and odor-free.

4. **Lighting and Temperature Check:**

Ensure all lights are functioning. Confirm basking and cool zone temperatures with a digital thermometer.

5. **Interaction and Observation:**

Gently interact with your dragon to build trust. Watch for changes in appetite, movement, behavior, or appearance.

Weekly Care Tasks

1. **Full Feeding Dish Cleaning:**

Wash food and water dishes with hot water and a reptile-safe disinfectant.

2. **Bathing (optional):**

Offer a warm bath for hydration, especially during shedding.

3. **Substrate and Decor Wipe Down:**

Clean surfaces with a reptile-safe cleaner to remove bacteria and debris.

4. **UVB Light Check:**

Confirm the bulb is still emitting UVB if you have a UV meter. Make sure there's no obstruction like dust or glass.

Monthly Care Tasks

1. **Deep Clean the Enclosure:**

Remove your dragon and thoroughly clean the entire tank, including hides, rocks, and climbing decor.

2. **Inspect UVB and Heat Bulbs:**

Replace UVB bulbs every 6–12 months even if they still emit light—UVB output diminishes over time.

3. **Health Check:**

Weigh your dragon and check for signs of parasites, stuck shed, or abnormal growth.

Care Task Table

Task	Frequency	Purpose
Feed appropriate diet	Daily	Provide nutrition for growth and health
Change and clean water bowl	Daily	Ensure hydration and prevent bacteria
Spot clean feces and debris	Daily	Maintain cleanliness and hygiene
Check lights and temperatures	Daily	Ensure correct heating and lighting
Observe behavior and appetite	Daily	Catch early signs of illness
Clean food and water dishes	Weekly	Prevent buildup of germs and biofilm
Bathe (optional)	Weekly	Assist with hydration and shedding
Wipe down surfaces and decor	Weekly	Minimize bacteria and maintain hygiene
Deep clean tank and accessories	Monthly	Sanitize full enclosure environment
Inspect/replace lighting	Monthly	Maintain effective UVB and heat output
Weigh and check overall health	Monthly	Monitor growth and detect early health issues

Conclusion

Routine care isn't just about keeping the enclosure tidy—it's about creating a stable, healthy environment for your bearded dragon to thrive. With a simple schedule of daily, weekly, and monthly tasks, you'll stay on top of their needs and build a bond rooted in trust and attentiveness.

Chapter 27
How to Handle a Bearded Dragon

Handling your bearded dragon is one of the most enjoyable parts of pet ownership—but it must be done correctly. Proper handling builds trust, strengthens your bond, and helps your dragon become more social and confident. On the other hand, poor or rough handling can lead to stress, injury, and even aggression.

In this chapter, you'll learn how to pick up, hold, and interact with your bearded dragon safely and respectfully.

Start with Trust

Before attempting to handle your dragon, make sure it feels comfortable in its environment. A dragon that has recently arrived or is still adjusting to a new enclosure should be given a few days to settle in. During this time, talk to it softly, move slowly around the enclosure, and let it see and smell your hand without physical contact.

Look for signs your dragon is relaxed: flat basking posture, clear eyes, calm movements, and interest in its surroundings.

How to Pick Up Your Dragon

1. Approach from the front or side

Avoid reaching from above. In the wild, predators come from above, and this can trigger fear. Always let your dragon see your hand approaching.

2. Use both hands

Slide your hand under its chest, just behind the front legs, and support its entire body—especially the tail—with your other hand. Never grab the tail or limbs.

3. Lift gently and slowly

Once supported, lift smoothly. Sudden or jerky motions can startle your dragon and cause it to leap or flail.

How to Hold Your Dragon

- Keep one hand under the body and allow your dragon to rest its front legs on your hand or wrist.
- Use your second hand to support the back legs and tail.
- Let it sit on your chest, shoulder, or lap, but always supervise closely.
- Hold them close to your body to provide security and warmth.

Your dragon may shift, explore, or lick your hand—this is normal curiosity, not aggression.

Signs of Stress While Handling

- Puffing or blackening beard
- Hissing or gaping mouth
- Darting or trying to flee
- Flailing limbs or tail whipping

If you see these signs, gently return your dragon to its enclosure and try again later. Always end handling sessions on a calm note to build positive associations.

Conclusion

Handling a bearded dragon isn't just about lifting them—it's about respecting their instincts, reading their signals, and moving with care. Done right, handling builds trust and turns your dragon into a calm, confident companion who enjoys spending time with you.

Chapter 28
Bathing and Shedding Help

Bearded dragons are relatively low-maintenance reptiles, but regular bathing and proper support during shedding are essential to their health and comfort. These routines help keep their skin clean, support hydration, and prevent complications such as retained shed or dehydration. Understanding when and how to bathe your dragon and how to assist with shedding will ensure your pet remains healthy and stress-free.

Why Bearded Dragons Need Baths

In the wild, bearded dragons absorb moisture through occasional contact with dew, rain, or water sources they find. In captivity, where humidity is kept low, weekly baths help compensate by offering hydration and encouraging healthy skin function.

Benefits of bathing:

- Promotes hydration through absorption or drinking
- Aids digestion and helps stimulate bowel movements
- Softens old skin to support clean shedding
- Cleans away dirt, feces, or food residue from the body

While not all dragons drink during baths, many enjoy soaking and may become noticeably calmer in warm water.

How to Bathe a Bearded Dragon

Bathing should always be done gently and with close supervision. Follow these steps to make the experience safe and positive:

1. **Use a shallow basin or sink:**

The water should be no deeper than your dragon's elbows when standing. Shallow plastic tubs, sinks, or storage bins work well.

2. **Water temperature:**

Use warm water (between 90°F and 100°F), similar to a baby's bath. Always check with a thermometer to avoid burns or chills.

3. **Bath duration:**

Soak your dragon for 10 to 20 minutes. If the water cools down too much, end the bath or replace it with warm water.

4. Cleaning:

You don't need soap. If your dragon has stuck shed or dirt, gently splash water or use your fingers to help loosen it. Never scrub aggressively.

5. Drying:

After the bath, gently pat your dragon dry with a clean towel. Always dry thoroughly before returning to the enclosure, especially if the tank is cooler or during colder months.

How Often Should You Bathe Them?

- **Juveniles:** 3 to 4 times per week
- **Adults:** 1 to 2 times per week
- **During shedding or brumation:** Increase to support hydration and help remove loose skin
- **Sick or constipated dragons:** Daily short baths may help, but consult a vet if symptoms persist

Avoid overbathing, especially for dragons that dislike water. Too many baths can dry out the skin, particularly if humidity is too low in the enclosure.

Shedding: What to Expect

Bearded dragons shed throughout their lives. Hatchlings and juveniles shed frequently—every few weeks—as they grow. Adults may shed only a few times a year, usually in patches such as the tail, legs, or face.

Signs of shedding:

- Dull or grayish skin before the shed
- Dry, flaky patches
- Decreased appetite
- Increased scratching, rubbing, or restlessness

Shedding is a normal process, and in most cases, dragons do not need help. However, there are times when gentle support is beneficial.

Helping With Shedding

Do:

- Offer regular warm baths to loosen skin
- Increase humidity slightly in the enclosure (but not above 40–50 percent)

- Gently rub soft, wet cloth over flaky areas during or after a bath
- Provide rough objects like branches or rocks for natural rubbing

Do not:

- Pull or peel off skin manually, even if it looks loose
- Use oils or lotions not designed for reptiles
- Over-mist or soak too often, which can lead to skin irritation or respiratory issues

If shed is stuck around the toes, tail tip, or eyes and does not loosen after a few baths, consult a reptile vet. Retained shed in these areas can restrict blood flow and lead to serious complications.

Conclusion

Bathing and shedding are natural, important parts of a bearded dragon's care. By making baths comfortable and supporting clean, stress-free sheds, you ensure your dragon's skin stays healthy and your pet feels refreshed and at ease. With gentle handling, proper hydration, and a clean, well-equipped enclosure, these routines will become easy habits that keep your dragon thriving.

Chapter 29
Vet Visits and Health Checks

Bearded dragons are hardy animals, but like all pets, they need regular health monitoring and occasional veterinary care. Unlike cats and dogs, reptiles often hide signs of illness until the condition becomes serious. That's why it's important to perform regular at-home health checks and schedule periodic visits with a **reptile-experienced veterinarian**.

This chapter will guide you through when to seek professional help, what to check at home, and how to recognize signs of illness early.

Finding the Right Vet

Not all veterinarians are trained to treat reptiles, so it's crucial to locate one who is experienced with exotic pets, specifically reptiles or lizards. Reptile vets understand the unique anatomy, metabolism, and care needs of bearded dragons and are more likely to catch subtle health problems early.

Ideally, schedule a **baseline wellness exam** within a few weeks of bringing your dragon home. This allows the vet to check for parasites, examine overall condition, and establish a health record for future reference.

When to Visit the Vet

You should seek veterinary care if your bearded dragon shows any of the following:

- Significant weight loss or bloating
- Sunken eyes or wrinkled, dry skin
- Lack of appetite for more than a few days
- Limping or difficulty moving
- Abnormal stool (diarrhea, blood, undigested food)
- Lethargy or unresponsiveness
- Labored breathing or open-mouth breathing (not while basking)
- Black beard that stays dark for long periods without cause
- Stuck shed around toes, tail, or eyes
- Vomiting or regurgitation
- Sores, swelling, or strange growths on the body

Early intervention can prevent minor issues from becoming life-threatening problems.

At-Home Health Checks

Make it a habit to do a simple visual inspection of your dragon every week. Look for:

- **Body condition:** A healthy dragon has a plump tail base and strong limbs.
- **Eyes:** Should be clear, bright, and alert.
- **Mouth:** Check for signs of rot, swelling, or discolored gums.
- **Skin:** Monitor for stuck shed, unusual bumps, wounds, or parasites.
- **Activity level:** Healthy dragons are alert, responsive, and explore their space.

Weigh your dragon once a month using a kitchen scale. Sudden drops in weight can indicate illness even if the dragon appears fine otherwise.

Conclusion

Routine health checks and vet visits are essential parts of responsible bearded dragon care. By staying observant and proactive, you help catch problems early, ensure your dragon lives a longer, healthier life, and deepen your understanding of their unique needs. Regular checkups are not just for emergencies—they are key to prevention and peace of mind.

Chapter 30
Cleaning the Tank

A clean enclosure is essential for your bearded dragon's health. Dirty tanks can harbor harmful bacteria, fungi, parasites, and unpleasant odors—all of which can affect your dragon's immune system and stress levels. Creating a regular cleaning routine not only keeps your dragon safe but also makes your home more pleasant and reduces the chances of illness.

Proper cleaning involves both **daily maintenance** and **deep cleaning** on a regular basis. Let's break it down.

Daily Cleaning Tasks

1. **Spot Clean Waste:**

Remove any feces, urates, uneaten food, and shed skin as soon as you see them. This prevents bacterial buildup and keeps odors down.

2. **Change Water:**

Dump, rinse, and refill the water dish with fresh, dechlorinated water daily. Dragons often walk through or defecate in their bowl.

3. **Wipe Visible Messes:**

If food or feces are smeared on surfaces or decor, wipe it up with a paper towel and a reptile-safe cleaner.

Weekly Cleaning Tasks

1. **Dish Cleaning:**

Food and water dishes should be scrubbed with hot water and mild dish soap or a reptile-safe disinfectant once a week.

2. **Surface Cleaning:**

Wipe down hides, hammocks, climbing branches, and tank walls with a diluted vinegar solution or reptile-safe spray. Allow them to dry before returning to the tank.

Monthly Deep Cleaning

1. **Remove Your Dragon:**

Gently place your dragon in a safe, temporary holding area like a clean bin or secure enclosure.

2. Remove All Accessories and Substrate:

Take out decor, substrate, and dishes. If you're using tile or reptile carpet, remove and wash thoroughly. Dispose of used paper towels or old loose substrate if applicable.

3. Disinfect the Enclosure:

Use a 10% bleach solution or reptile-safe disinfectant to clean the inside of the tank. Rinse well with water and let it air dry completely.

4. Clean and Replace Items:

Scrub and rinse all hides, branches, and rocks. Ensure they are dry and free of soap or cleaner residue before placing them back.

Conclusion

Consistent cleaning is a small effort with big rewards. It helps prevent illness, reduces stress, and gives your dragon a safe, healthy home where it can thrive. A clean habitat is the foundation of great bearded dragon care.

Part 7
Health and Common Issues

Chapter 31
Signs of a Healthy Beardie

A healthy bearded dragon is alert, active, and responsive to its surroundings. While they may not be expressive in the same way as dogs or cats, they give clear signals when they're thriving. Learning to recognize these signs will help you confidently monitor your dragon's well-being and catch any early signs of trouble.

Here's what to look for in a happy, healthy beardie:

1. Bright, Clear Eyes

Healthy dragons have wide-open, alert eyes with no crustiness or swelling. They should track movement and respond to your presence. Dull or sunken eyes may signal dehydration, illness, or fatigue.

2. Strong Appetite

A good appetite is a strong indicator of health. While dragons in brumation or shedding may eat less, a healthy beardie will generally show enthusiasm for meals—especially insects and favorite greens.

3. Smooth, Even Shedding

Shedding is normal at all life stages. A healthy dragon will shed in patches with no signs of retained skin around the toes, tail, or eyes. If your dragon sheds regularly and cleanly, its skin is growing and renewing properly.

4. Well-Formed Stool

Normal dragon droppings are firm and dark with a white urate cap (the reptile version of urine). Runny, discolored, or unusually smelly stool may suggest parasites or dietary issues.

5. Regular Activity and Alertness

Healthy beardies are active during the day. They bask, explore, climb, and react to changes in their environment. A calm dragon may rest often, but it should still respond when you approach or offer food.

6. Good Body Condition

A healthy bearded dragon has a full, rounded tail base, strong limbs, and no visible bones or sunken areas. Its body should feel firm, not bloated or overly soft.

7. Clean, Clear Nose and Mouth

There should be no mucus, bubbling, or discoloration. Breathing should be silent and smooth, even during basking.

Conclusion

Knowing what a healthy bearded dragon looks and acts like helps you build confidence as a keeper. When your dragon displays these signs consistently, you can be sure you're providing the care it needs to live a long, happy life.

Chapter 32
Parasites and Infections

Even with excellent care, bearded dragons can be vulnerable to internal parasites and external infections. Many parasites exist in small amounts in a dragon's digestive tract without causing issues, but when populations grow or the immune system weakens, they can lead to serious health problems. Infections—whether respiratory, bacterial, or fungal—can also take hold in unsanitary or stressful conditions.

This chapter outlines the most common parasites and infections seen in bearded dragons, their symptoms, and how to manage or prevent them.

Common Internal Parasites

1. **Pinworms:**

These are the most common internal parasites. Small numbers may not cause harm, but large infestations can lead to weight loss, diarrhea, or lethargy.

2. **Coccidia:**

A protozoan parasite that can cause diarrhea, poor growth, and appetite loss. Coccidia spreads through contaminated feces and is especially common in young or newly acquired dragons.

3. **Other worms (hookworms, tapeworms):**

Less common but potentially serious. These can enter through contaminated feeders or substrate.

Symptoms of internal parasites:

- Runny, foul-smelling stool
- Weight loss despite a normal appetite
- Lethargy or bloating
- Reduced growth in juveniles

A fecal exam by a reptile vet is the only reliable way to diagnose internal parasites. Many are easily treated with prescription medications once identified.

External Parasites

1. **Mites:**

These tiny parasites can hide under scales or near the eyes and mouth. They may appear as black or red specks.

2. **Ticks:**

Less common but possible, especially in wild-caught dragons or contaminated enclosures.

Signs of external parasites:

- Constant scratching or rubbing
- Visible dots on the skin
- Soaking in the water bowl more than usual

Treatment includes special reptile-safe sprays and deep cleaning of the enclosure.

Infections to Watch For

1. **Respiratory Infections:**

Caused by poor ventilation, high humidity, or cold temperatures.

Signs include:

- Wheezing or clicking noises
- Mucus around the nose or mouth
- Open-mouth breathing when not basking
- Lethargy and lack of appetite

2. **Mouth Rot (Infectious Stomatitis):**

A bacterial infection of the gums or jaw.

Look for:

- Swollen or discolored gums
- Refusal to eat
- Pus or mucus in the mouth

3. **Skin Infections (bacterial or fungal):**

Can result from injuries, dirty conditions, or stuck shed.

Symptoms:

- Discolored patches
- Oozing sores or rough, crusty skin

- Swelling in localized areas

Prevention Tips

- Maintain clean enclosures with regular spot and deep cleaning
- Quarantine new reptiles for at least 30 days before introducing them to others
- Avoid wild-caught insects or unknown food sources
- Monitor humidity and temperature closely
- Keep up with regular vet visits and fecal exams (ideally twice per year)

Conclusion

Parasites and infections are common but preventable aspects of reptile care. By staying alert to changes in behavior, appearance, and waste, and by maintaining excellent hygiene, you can catch issues early and keep your bearded dragon safe, healthy, and comfortable. Prompt veterinary treatment and good husbandry are your strongest defenses.

Chapter 33
Metabolic Bone Disease (MBD)

Metabolic Bone Disease, often abbreviated as MBD, is one of the most common and preventable illnesses in captive bearded dragons. It occurs when the body is unable to properly absorb and use calcium, usually due to **poor UVB lighting**, **calcium deficiency**, or an **imbalanced calcium-to-phosphorus ratio** in the diet.

When calcium is lacking, the body pulls it from the bones, leading to weakened skeletal structure, deformities, and in severe cases, paralysis or death. Young dragons are especially vulnerable during rapid growth stages.

Symptoms of MBD:

- Soft or swollen jaw and limbs
- Difficulty walking or dragging limbs
- Muscle twitching or tremors
- Curved spine or tail
- Loss of appetite and lethargy
- Visible deformities in the jaw or back

MBD often progresses gradually, so early detection is key. Any sign of limb weakness or odd posture should prompt an immediate vet visit.

Causes:

- Lack of **UVB lighting** or expired UVB bulbs
- Insufficient **calcium supplementation**
- Feeding foods high in **phosphorus** without balancing calcium
- Excessive **oxalates** in the diet, which block calcium absorption
- No access to proper **heat** for digestion and nutrient processing

Prevention:

- Use a high-quality **T5 UVB bulb** and replace it every 6–12 months
- Dust feeder insects with **calcium powder** 4–5 times per week
- Provide a **balanced diet** of greens, veggies, and appropriate insects
- Maintain correct **basking temperatures** to aid digestion

Conclusion

Metabolic Bone Disease is serious but entirely avoidable with proper care. By prioritizing calcium, UVB exposure, and a balanced diet, you protect your bearded dragon from pain, deformity, and long-term health issues. Prevention is always easier—and more effective—than treatment.

Chapter 34
Impaction and Dehydration

Two of the most common and dangerous health issues in bearded dragons are **impaction** and **dehydration**. Both can develop silently over time and lead to severe complications if not addressed early. Fortunately, with the right care and awareness, both conditions are preventable.

Impaction: What It Is and Why It Happens

Impaction occurs when your dragon's digestive tract becomes blocked. This can be caused by the ingestion of indigestible materials, excessive feeder size, or a lack of hydration and proper heat for digestion. If left untreated, impaction can lead to paralysis, organ failure, or death.

Common causes of impaction:

- **Loose substrate:** Sand, crushed walnut shell, gravel, or wood chips are all dangerous. If accidentally ingested, they can clump together inside the digestive system.
- **Oversized insects:** Feeding prey that's too large—especially hard-bodied insects like superworms—can clog the intestines.
- **Low temperatures:** Digestion depends on proper basking temperatures (95–110°F). Without it, food moves slowly or not at all.
- **Lack of hydration:** Dehydration causes dry, hard stool, which becomes difficult to pass.

Symptoms of impaction:

- Lack of bowel movements for several days
- Swollen or bloated abdomen
- Lethargy and lack of appetite
- Dragging back legs or partial paralysis
- Straining or discomfort when trying to pass stool

What to do:

- Give your dragon a warm bath to help relax the muscles
- Gently massage the lower belly in circular motions
- Check temperatures and enclosure setup
- If symptoms persist beyond 48 hours, visit a reptile veterinarian

Dehydration: Subtle But Serious

Bearded dragons are desert animals, but that doesn't mean they don't need water. In captivity, where humidity is often controlled, dehydration can occur more easily than you might think—especially if your dragon isn't getting enough water through food or misting.

Signs of dehydration:

- Wrinkled, sagging skin
- Sunken eyes
- Lethargy or sluggish behavior
- Lack of appetite
- Hard or dry stool

Causes of dehydration:

- Inadequate water intake (not drinking from the bowl)
- Lack of moisture-rich foods (like greens or squash)
- Excessive heat without humidity balance
- Illness or stress reducing drinking behavior

How to rehydrate your dragon:

- **Offer a shallow water bowl** daily and refresh it often
- **Mist the snout** lightly and see if your dragon licks the water
- **Provide warm baths** 1–3 times a week (especially during shedding)
- Feed **moist vegetables and fruits** in moderation
- Monitor the humidity—ideal levels should stay between 30% and 40%

If dehydration persists despite these efforts, consult a reptile vet. Chronic dehydration can lead to organ strain, constipation, and even impaction.

Prevention Tips

- Always offer **appropriate substrate**—use tile, reptile carpet, or paper
- Maintain a **proper temperature gradient** with a reliable basking area
- Feed **insects no larger than the space between your dragon's eyes**
- Offer **hydrating baths** and misting as needed

- Observe your dragon's **bowel habits** and energy levels
- Keep track of weight and body condition monthly

Conclusion

Impaction and dehydration are both preventable with consistent care and observation. Understanding how to identify early warning signs and maintaining a well-balanced environment will go a long way in protecting your bearded dragon from these silent but serious health risks. A hydrated dragon with good digestion is a healthy, happy dragon.

Chapter 35
First Aid and Emergency Tips

Even with the best care, accidents and health issues can happen. While a veterinarian should always be your first point of contact for serious problems, it's essential to be prepared for basic first aid and emergency situations. Knowing how to respond calmly and effectively can make a huge difference in your bearded dragon's recovery.

Basic First Aid Kit for Bearded Dragons

Keep a small reptile-specific first aid kit on hand with the following:

- Digital thermometer and humidity gauge
- Tweezers (for removing debris or insects)
- Saline solution (for flushing eyes or wounds)
- Betadine or chlorhexidine (for cleaning cuts)
- Cotton swabs and gauze pads
- Reptile-safe electrolyte or hydration fluids (like diluted Pedialyte)
- Feeding syringe (for fluids or emergency feeding)
- Critical care formula (vet-recommended, for sick or underweight dragons)

Common Situations and What to Do

1. Minor Cuts or Scrapes:

Clean gently with diluted betadine or saline. Keep the area dry and monitor for signs of infection like swelling or pus. Avoid using human antiseptic creams.

2. Burns (from bulbs or surfaces):

Cool the area with a lukewarm saline rinse. Apply nothing unless directed by a vet. Adjust bulb placement to prevent recurrence.

3. Impaction:

Give a warm bath and gently massage the lower abdomen. If there's no bowel movement within 48 hours or your dragon seems distressed, call a vet.

4. Dehydration:

Offer oral fluids using a dropper or syringe. Provide warm baths. If your dragon is unresponsive, seek immediate veterinary care.

5. Severe Injury or Paralysis:

If your dragon is dragging limbs, not moving, or has fallen from a height, limit movement by placing it in a padded container and transport to a vet as soon as possible.

Emergency Contacts

Always have the contact information of a **reptile-experienced veterinarian** on hand. Know the location and hours of the nearest emergency clinic that handles exotic animals.

Conclusion

In an emergency, quick action, a calm approach, and basic knowledge can stabilize your bearded dragon before professional help arrives. Being prepared doesn't just show love—it can save a life.

Part 8
Comparing Bearded Dragons with Other Reptiles

Chapter 36
Bearded Dragons vs Geckos

Comparing Two Popular Pet Reptiles

Here's a side-by-side comparison of bearded dragons and geckos (specifically leopard geckos, the most common gecko kept as a pet), across key care and behavior categories:

Category	Bearded Dragon	Leopard Gecko
Size & Appearance	18–24 inches; broad body with spiky "beard" and expressive eyes	7–10 inches; slender body with smooth skin and prominent eyes
Temperament	Docile, social, and often enjoys handling	Calm but more solitary; tolerates handling but prefers less
Habitat Needs	Large enclosure (75–120+ gallons); needs UVB and high heat	Smaller enclosure (20–40 gallons); no UVB required, moderate heat
Activity Pattern	Diurnal (active during the day)	Nocturnal (active in the evening and night)
Diet	Omnivore: insects, greens, vegetables	Insectivore: mostly crickets, mealworms, and other feeders
Ease of Care	Moderate; more hands-on due to lighting and feeding needs	Beginner-friendly; simpler setup and lower maintenance

This table highlights that while both species make excellent pets, bearded dragons are more interactive and engaging during the day, whereas geckos require less space and are ideal for quieter environments and nighttime observation.

Chapter 37
Bearded Dragons vs Iguanas
Understanding the Key Differences Between Two Popular Pet Lizards

Bearded dragons and iguanas are both fascinating reptiles, but they differ greatly in terms of care, temperament, and suitability for most pet owners. The table below compares the two across major categories:

Category	Bearded Dragon	Green Iguana
Size & Appearance	Medium-sized (18–24 inches); stocky with spiked beard	Very large (4–6 feet); long body with tail and prominent dewlap
Temperament	Docile, social, often enjoys human interaction	Territorial, can be aggressive; generally not beginner-friendly
Habitat Needs	75–120+ gallon tank; needs UVB, basking zone, and dry climate	Requires a very large enclosure (room-sized); high humidity and UVB
Activity Pattern	Diurnal (active during the day)	Diurnal
Diet	Omnivore: insects, greens, vegetables	Strict herbivore: leafy greens, vegetables, fruits
Ease of Care	Moderate; good for beginners with proper setup	High maintenance; not recommended for first-time reptile keepers

Bearded dragons are manageable, interactive, and make ideal pet reptiles for families and beginners. Iguanas, on the other hand, require advanced care, large space, and significant commitment. Choose wisely based on your lifestyle, experience, and space.

Chapter 38
Are Bearded Dragons Good Beginner Reptiles?

Yes, in many ways, bearded dragons are one of the most beginner-friendly reptiles available today. They strike a unique balance between ease of care, tolerance for handling, and interactive behavior that is hard to match.

1. Friendly Disposition

Bearded dragons are famously calm. Unlike many reptiles that dislike handling, most beardies tolerate or even enjoy being held. With regular, gentle interaction, they become accustomed to their owner and often relax on a shoulder or lap without fuss.

This temperament makes them suitable for adults, children (with supervision), and anyone new to reptiles who may feel nervous around more active or defensive species.

2. Manageable Size and Setup

An adult bearded dragon grows to about 18 to 24 inches in length. While they do need a large enclosure (ideally 75 to 120 gallons), their size is not overwhelming. They are easier to house than an iguana or monitor lizard and more interactive than smaller reptiles like leopard geckos.

Their habitat requires a heat source, UVB lighting, proper substrate, and daily feeding, but it is not overly complex for someone willing to do basic research and maintenance.

3. Diurnal Activity

Bearded dragons are active during the day, aligning with human schedules. This makes them easier to observe and interact with compared to nocturnal reptiles like leopard geckos, who are most alert at night.

A bearded dragon's routine of basking, exploring, and eating during daylight hours makes them engaging and rewarding pets, especially for those who enjoy watching natural behavior unfold.

4. Educational Value

For families or classrooms, bearded dragons offer a hands-on learning opportunity. Their diet changes as they grow, they shed visibly, and they display fascinating body language. They help teach responsibility, observation skills, and respect for animals.

5. Moderate Maintenance

While they do require daily care and some initial setup investment, bearded dragons are not overly high-maintenance. Once the habitat is properly established with heating and lighting, most care revolves around feeding, cleaning, and interaction.

For first-time reptile owners willing to learn and commit, bearded dragons are a practical and rewarding choice.

Chapter 39
How Bearded Dragons Differ in Intelligence and Temperament

Bearded dragons stand out among reptiles not just for their looks, but for their surprisingly responsive and observant nature. They may not learn tricks like a dog or solve puzzles like a parrot, but their intelligence is evident in the way they navigate their environment and interact with people.

1. Social Awareness

Unlike many reptiles that prefer to be left alone, bearded dragons often appear curious about their surroundings. They watch movement, respond to voices, and learn routines. With time, they recognize their keeper's face and may move toward the front of the tank at feeding times or when they see a familiar person.

Other reptiles, like leopard geckos and corn snakes, tend to be more reactive and instinct-driven. They may learn patterns, but they typically do not demonstrate the same level of visual engagement.

2. Body Language and Expression

Bearded dragons use a rich set of gestures to communicate. You will see head bobbing, arm waving, beard puffing, and tail curling—all forms of body language that reflect mood, social status, and even territorial instincts.

These visual cues make it easier for owners to understand their dragon's comfort level. Other reptiles, such as snakes, may show stress or threat only through hissing or fleeing, offering less clear communication.

3. Trainability

While training reptiles is never as straightforward as with mammals, bearded dragons have shown potential to be trained for basic tasks. Some owners successfully teach them to come when called, accept handling more easily, or follow a target for feeding.

This is largely due to their calm nature and strong food motivation. Compare this to more high-strung reptiles like iguanas, which can become aggressive, or crepuscular species like ball pythons, which are typically uninterested in interaction.

4. Emotional Range and Behavior

Bearded dragons can appear to express a variety of moods—from alert and curious to defensive or sleepy. They show a preference for warmth and comfort, may react differently to strangers, and sometimes settle in for a nap in their owner's lap.

While these are instinctual behaviors, the frequency and range of expression in bearded dragons makes them feel more connected and relatable than many other reptiles.

5. Problem-Solving and Exploration

Beardies display basic problem-solving skills. When placed in new environments, they explore, climb, and navigate barriers. They are known to investigate food sources creatively, and some seem to adapt quickly to changes in enclosure layout or enrichment.

Compare this to species that rely on rigid instinctual behavior or freeze when faced with novelty. Bearded dragons are more flexible and curious, traits that make them particularly fun to observe.

Conclusion

Bearded dragons are excellent beginner reptiles thanks to their calm demeanor, manageable care needs, and active daytime behavior. But they are more than just easy pets—they are smart, expressive, and surprisingly interactive. Their ability to recognize patterns, respond to people, and communicate through body language places them among the most personable reptiles available today.

Whether you are a first-time keeper or an experienced reptile enthusiast, a bearded dragon offers the unique experience of sharing your space with a creature that observes you right back—and seems to understand more than you might expect.

Part 9
Bonding & Enrichment

Chapter 40
Do They Recognize Their Owners?

Yes, your bearded dragon can recognize you—and over time, it may even show clear signs of preference toward you over strangers. While bearded dragons don't form emotional bonds the way mammals do, they are observant, intelligent reptiles capable of learning routines, faces, and voices.

You might notice that your dragon behaves differently around you than it does with others. It may relax more when you're near, climb onto your hand without hesitation, or watch you move across the room. These are signs of recognition and trust. Bearded dragons associate you with safety, warmth, and food, all of which contribute to their comfort.

They rely heavily on visual and scent cues. Over time, they learn your appearance, the sound of your voice, and even your scent. If you've been consistent with feeding, gentle handling, and calm interaction, your dragon likely sees you as a familiar, non-threatening presence in their world.

While your dragon won't wag its tail or run to greet you like a dog might, it may express recognition through subtler behaviors—like approaching the front of the tank when you enter the room or calmly climbing onto your hand. These actions reflect comfort and awareness, even if they're not driven by emotion in the same way human-animal relationships usually work.

Consistency and patience are key. The more calm, positive experiences your dragon has with you, the stronger the recognition becomes. So, while your bearded dragon may not love you in the traditional sense, it certainly knows who you are—and that's the beginning of trust.

Chapter 41
How to Build Trust

Building trust with your bearded dragon is the foundation of a rewarding and stress-free relationship. While they may not show affection like mammals, bearded dragons are intelligent, observant, and capable of recognizing their owners over time. Gaining their trust takes patience, consistency, and gentle handling.

Start Slow and Be Present

When you first bring your dragon home, give it a few days to settle into its new environment. During this time, avoid handling and instead focus on letting your dragon get used to your presence. Sit near the enclosure, speak softly, and move slowly. This helps your dragon associate you with calm, non-threatening energy.

Approach Gently

Always approach from the side or front—never from above. In nature, predators attack from above, and quick overhead movements can trigger a fear response. Move your hand slowly into the tank and allow your dragon to see you coming. Offer your hand near its side to give it a chance to investigate.

Hand Feeding

Feeding by hand is one of the quickest ways to build positive associations. Try offering small pieces of greens or favorite insects from your fingers or palm. Your dragon will start linking your hand with safety and food.

Short Handling Sessions

Once your dragon seems calm around you, begin handling it in short sessions. Support its entire body with both hands, and let it rest on your chest, lap, or arm. Keep sessions brief at first, gradually increasing the time as your dragon becomes more comfortable.

Routine and Respect

Stick to a consistent schedule for feeding and interaction. Dragons feel more secure when they know what to expect. Always return your dragon to the enclosure gently and avoid handling during shedding or brumation, when they may be more sensitive.

Conclusion

Trust is earned over time through gentle, respectful interaction. With patience, your bearded dragon will come to see you as a calm and predictable presence, turning everyday care into a bonding experience.

Chapter 42
Games and Toys They Enjoy

Bearded dragons may not play in the same way as dogs or cats, but they are intelligent and curious creatures that benefit from mental and physical stimulation. Incorporating playtime into your dragon's routine not only keeps them active but also strengthens your bond.

Let's explore some games and toy ideas that encourage natural behavior and bring out your dragon's playful side.

1. Insect Chase

Live feeder insects like crickets or dubia roaches provide excellent exercise and mental stimulation. Watching and chasing prey mimics natural hunting behavior. Use a separate feeding bin or a sectioned area in the tank to allow for safe, contained chasing. Always supervise, and remove any uneaten insects to prevent biting.

2. Foraging Games

Hiding small bits of food around the enclosure encourages your dragon to explore and sniff out their treats. You can use shallow dishes, hollow logs, or even safe fabric folds. Place pieces of fruit or greens in different locations and watch your dragon search them out.

3. Food Puzzle Toys

While designed for small mammals or birds, some puzzle toys can be repurposed for dragons. A clean wiffle ball filled with greens or worms can be rolled around, prompting your dragon to chase and extract the food. You can also try a shallow, non-toxic digging box with bits of food mixed into the substrate.

4. Climbing Challenges

Bearded dragons love to climb. Rearranging logs, hammocks, and rocks can provide a new "adventure course" within their tank. Try adjusting decor weekly to add novelty and keep your dragon curious.

5. Tactile Toys

Some dragons enjoy textured objects, like soft plastic balls, clean rubber chew toys, or small stuffed animals (without buttons or loose threads). While they don't "play" with them as dogs do, they may explore or climb on them, especially outside the tank.

6. Mirror Play (With Caution)

Occasionally, a dragon may become intrigued or stimulated by seeing its reflection. A small hand mirror can create a temporary curiosity session. However, extended exposure may cause stress, especially in males. Use sparingly and watch for signs of agitation.

7. Supervised Outside Time

Letting your dragon explore a safe, enclosed area outside the tank can be one of the best forms of play. Use a secure playpen, patio, or sunny indoor spot. Always supervise and avoid exposure to chemicals, other pets, or overheating.

Conclusion

Bearded dragons enjoy stimulation when it taps into their natural instincts—hunting, climbing, exploring, and observing. Providing enrichment through toys and simple games not only enhances their quality of life but also makes them more active, curious, and confident companions.

Chapter 43
Training and Exploring with Your Gecko

At the same time,

Let's explore how to do both safely and successfully.

Chapter 43: Safe Outdoor Exploration

Spending time outside the tank is one of the most enriching experiences you can give your bearded dragon. Whether it's a sun-soaked afternoon in the backyard or a supervised crawl across the living room carpet, exploring new environments engages your dragon's senses and offers valuable stimulation. With proper precautions, you can even enjoy short outdoor adventures together.

Letting your bearded dragon enjoy the outdoors is a great way to simulate natural conditions, especially exposure to **real sunlight**, which provides **unfiltered UVB**—something even the best indoor bulbs can't fully replicate.

But the outdoors also come with risks. You'll need to take steps to ensure your dragon's adventure is fun, not frightening or dangerous.

Benefits of Outdoor Time

- **Natural UVB Exposure:** Boosts vitamin D3 production and supports bone health
- **Exercise:** Encourages walking, climbing, and natural movement
- **Mental Stimulation:** New sights, sounds, and smells promote alertness and curiosity
- **Bonding Time:** Being with you in a new setting strengthens trust

How to Prepare

1. Choose the Right Time and Weather

Avoid chilly or extremely hot days. Ideal outdoor temperatures range between 80°F and 90°F. Don't take your dragon out when the ground is too cold, or during direct midday heat in summer.

2. Create a Safe Space

A small, enclosed pet playpen with a mesh top works well for outdoor lounging. You can also use a leash and harness made specifically for reptiles. Never let your dragon roam freely—it can disappear quickly or fall prey to birds, cats, or dogs.

3. Avoid Chemical Exposure

Only place your dragon on untreated grass. Lawn fertilizers, weed killers, and pesticides can be deadly. Also avoid areas where other animals have urinated or defecated.

4. Always Supervise

Even a well-behaved dragon can bolt if startled. Keep your eyes on them at all times and be ready to intervene if they show signs of stress, like puffing their beard, freezing, or trying to dig.

5. Limit Exposure Time

Start with 10–15 minute sessions. Once your dragon adjusts, you can extend the time gradually, but always check for signs of overheating or stress.

Chapter 44
Training Tricks (Yes, It's Possible!)

You may not think of your bearded dragon as trainable, but they are surprisingly receptive to routine and repetition. While they may not learn tricks like a dog, they are capable of **associative learning**—recognizing patterns and connecting your actions with outcomes like food, safety, or comfort.

Bearded dragons are more capable than many owners realize—they can be trained to respond to their name, come when called, and even learn simple routines. With consistency and patience, training is not only possible, but also deeply rewarding.

Why Train a Bearded Dragon?

- Builds trust and confidence
- Enhances mental stimulation
- Encourages gentle, cooperative behavior
- Helps in practical ways (like coming when called or accepting handling)

Trick 1: Name Recognition

Bearded dragons can learn to associate their name with positive experiences, especially food. Say your dragon's name in a calm, clear voice each time you approach, feed, or interact with them.

How to train:

- Use their name during feeding (example: "Cleo, time to eat")
- Pair the sound with a favorite treat
- Be consistent—use the same tone and words each time

Over time, your dragon will begin to look toward you or approach the front of the tank when they hear their name.

Trick 2: Coming When Called

Once name recognition is strong, you can begin teaching your dragon to come toward you on cue.

How to train:

- Sit near your dragon at floor level
- Say their name and offer a visible treat or feeder insect
- Reward them only when they move toward you

Repeat a few times per session. Over days or weeks, they will begin to associate your voice and gesture with a reward and will respond more quickly.

Trick 3: Target Training

Target training uses a small object (like a colored stick or spoon) to direct your dragon's movement. It can be helpful for leading them out of the enclosure or toward a feeding spot.

How to train:

- Hold out the target and let your dragon investigate
- When they touch or follow it, reward with a treat
- Repeat and gradually move the target farther away

With practice, your dragon will follow the target on command.

Trick 4: Hand Climbing

If your dragon is hesitant to climb onto your hand, you can turn it into a trained behavior.

How to train:

- Gently place your hand in front of your dragon, palm up
- Use a treat to lure them forward
- Reward once all four legs are on your hand
- Keep sessions short and end on a calm note

This builds trust and makes regular handling easier and more enjoyable.

Training Tips

- **Use rewards:** Tiny pieces of fruit, hornworms, or dubia roaches work well
- **Keep sessions short:** 5–10 minutes is enough for a single lesson
- **Be consistent:** Same cue words, tone, and gestures help them learn faster
- **Be patient:** Dragons learn at their own pace. Never force or scold
- **Watch for stress:** If your dragon blacks its beard, freezes, or hides, end the session and try again another day

Conclusion

Outdoor exploration and basic training aren't just fun—they're essential for enriching your bearded dragon's life. By offering new environments and engaging your dragon in simple, rewarding activities, you support both their mental and physical health. Whether you're soaking up the sun together or watching them respond to your voice, these moments strengthen the bond you share and make dragon-keeping even more fulfilling.

Part 10
Breeding & Baby Beardies

Chapter 45
Breeding Behavior and Mating Process

Breeding bearded dragons can be a fascinating experience, but it also requires careful planning, a deep understanding of their behavior, and responsible care. The mating process involves a series of unique and sometimes intense behaviors that reflect natural instincts. If you're considering breeding your dragons—or even housing males and females together—it's important to know what to expect.

Breeding Season and Triggers

In the wild, bearded dragons breed during the warmer months after brumation (a hibernation-like rest period). In captivity, they may breed at any time of year, but spring and early summer tend to trigger natural hormonal changes due to increasing daylight and warmth.

To prepare for breeding, both the male and female should be at least **18 months old**, healthy, and of adequate weight. Breeding dragons too young can lead to complications, especially for females, whose bodies may not be ready to produce and lay eggs safely.

Courtship Behavior

Once in proximity, the male begins his courtship display. He may:

- **Bob his head rapidly** to show dominance
- **Blacken his beard**, making himself appear larger and more intimidating
- **Circle the female** and may twitch or stomp his front feet
- **Lick or nudge the female's side** to show interest

In response, a receptive female often **slowly waves her arm** in a circular motion and may crouch slightly, signaling submission. If she's not ready, she may run, puff up, or even nip back.

The Mating Process

When the female signals readiness, the male quickly mounts her from behind. He uses his mouth to grip the back of her neck or shoulders to hold her in place—this may look rough, but it is normal. The tails of both dragons curve to allow cloacal alignment, and mating lasts only a few minutes.

After mating, the male may continue to display dominant behaviors for a short while. At this point, it's best to **separate the pair** to prevent stress, overbreeding, or injury. Males can become aggressive or overzealous if left with the female too long.

Post-Mating Behavior

The female may show signs of being gravid (carrying eggs) within two to three weeks. Common signs include:

- Swollen, rounded belly
- Increased digging or restless behavior
- Decreased appetite
- Seeking warm or dark hiding spots

Provide a **lay box** filled with moist substrate such as damp soil or sand, where she can dig and lay her eggs comfortably. Failing to do so can lead to egg-binding, a serious and potentially fatal condition.

After laying, the female may bury the eggs and return to normal behavior. You should separate the eggs if you plan to incubate them, and ensure the female has access to calcium-rich food and time to recover.

Ethical Considerations

Breeding should only be done responsibly. Avoid breeding dragons with unknown health issues or closely related bloodlines. Always ensure you have a plan for the eggs—whether that's incubation or rehoming the hatchlings.

Conclusion

The bearded dragon mating process is instinctive, energetic, and sometimes intense. By preparing your dragons properly, understanding their behaviors, and respecting their needs before and after mating, you ensure a safer, healthier experience for both reptiles. Responsible breeding begins with education and care at every step.

Chapter 46
Laying Eggs and Incubation

Once a female bearded dragon has mated, she may begin developing eggs within a few weeks. This period, known as being gravid, is physically demanding and requires close observation and support from you. Whether the eggs are fertile or not, the process of laying them and, if applicable, incubating them correctly, is essential to the health of the mother and the success of the clutch.

Signs Your Female is Gravid

After successful mating, or sometimes even without mating (as females can lay infertile eggs), your bearded dragon may show signs such as:

- A noticeably swollen abdomen with visible egg shapes when viewed from above
- Restlessness and pacing
- Frequent digging, especially in corners or substrate
- Decreased appetite or refusal to eat
- Spending more time in cooler or hidden areas

As the eggs develop, her body will look fuller, especially around the lower belly. You may feel firm, marble-sized lumps through gentle abdominal palpation, though this should only be done if you're confident and careful.

Creating a Lay Box

A lay box gives your dragon a safe, appropriate space to deposit her eggs. Without one, she may retain the eggs, which can lead to egg-binding—a life-threatening condition.

How to set up a lay box:

- Use a large plastic container or tub that fits inside the enclosure or can be placed in a quiet, warm area
- Fill it with moist substrate, such as dampened play sand or a soil-sand mix, 6–10 inches deep
- Substrate should be firm enough to hold a tunnel but soft enough to dig
- Keep the lay box warm (around 85–90°F) and ensure the area is private and calm

The female will dig a tunnel, lay the eggs, then cover them. Once she's finished, remove her gently and place her back in her enclosure to rest and rehydrate.

After Laying: Post-Care for the Female

Laying a clutch can be exhausting. Afterward, provide:

- Extra hydration through a shallow bath
- High-calcium foods such as collard greens and calcium-dusted insects
- A quiet, clean enclosure where she can recover
- Monitor her for signs of infection, lethargy, or retained eggs. If you suspect any complications, consult a reptile vet immediately.

Incubating the Eggs

If the eggs are fertile and you plan to hatch them, proper incubation is crucial.

Steps for incubation:

1. **Remove the eggs carefully** from the lay box. Do not rotate them, as this can harm the developing embryo.
2. **Place eggs in an incubation container** (such as a deli cup or plastic tub with a lid), filled with a moist incubation medium like vermiculite or perlite.
3. **Humidity should be high** (80–90%), but the substrate should not be soaking wet. You want a damp, spongy feel.
4. **Temperature should stay steady** between 82–86°F. Use a reptile egg incubator for precise control.
5. **Monitor regularly** for mold, dehydration, or collapse. Slight dimpling late in incubation is normal.

Incubation takes about **55–75 days**, depending on temperature. Eggs should not be moved or disturbed once placed.

Conclusion

Egg-laying and incubation are delicate processes that require preparation, patience, and care. By providing your bearded dragon with the right environment and support, you help her pass through this natural event safely—and if the eggs are fertile, you may even get to welcome a new generation of baby dragons into the world.

Chapter 47
Caring for Hatchlings

Caring for bearded dragon hatchlings is both exciting and delicate. These tiny dragons, only about 3 to 4 inches long at birth, require special attention to ensure healthy growth and survival during their first few weeks of life. With the right setup, nutrition, and care, hatchlings can thrive and grow into strong juveniles.

Housing Hatchlings

Each hatchling needs space to move freely and bask without overcrowding. It's best to start with a small group of no more than five hatchlings per enclosure to reduce competition and stress.

Enclosure setup:

- Use a 20-gallon tank for small groups, with paper towel substrate to avoid impaction
- Basking spot: 105–110°F
- Cool side: 80–85°F
- UVB lighting is essential from day one
- Provide low hides and small climbing branches for security and stimulation

Avoid loose substrate, as hatchlings are prone to accidental ingestion.

Feeding Hatchlings

Young dragons have rapid metabolisms and should be fed multiple times daily. Insects make up the majority of their diet early on.

Feeding guidelines:

- Offer tiny crickets or black soldier fly larvae **3–5 times per day**
- Insects should be no larger than the space between the dragon's eyes
- Dust insects with **calcium powder daily** and multivitamins twice per week
- Introduce finely chopped greens (like dandelion or collard greens) from the start, even if ignored at first

Always remove uneaten insects to prevent them from nipping at your hatchlings.

Hydration and Shedding

Provide a shallow water dish and mist lightly once a day. Some hatchlings will drink water droplets from the sides of the tank or their snout. Regular shedding is common due to fast growth—warm baths can help loosen old skin if needed.

Monitoring Health

Watch for:

- Steady weight gain
- Clear eyes and alert behavior
- Regular eating and bowel movements

If a hatchling appears lethargic, stops eating, or shows signs of deformity or injury, isolate it and consult a reptile vet.

Conclusion

The hatchling stage sets the foundation for a bearded dragon's health and behavior. With consistent warmth, food, and gentle care, you'll help your young dragons grow strong and confident from their very first days.

Chapter 48
Breeding Ethics and Responsibilities

Breeding bearded dragons can be a rewarding experience, but it also comes with significant responsibility. While producing baby dragons may sound exciting, ethical breeding requires more than simply pairing two reptiles. It demands planning, commitment, and a long-term vision for the health and well-being of both the parents and their offspring.

Before you begin, it's essential to evaluate whether breeding is the right choice—for you, your animals, and the wider reptile community.

Know Your Purpose

Ask yourself: *Why am I breeding?*

If your goal is to improve genetics, preserve a healthy bloodline, or offer responsibly raised dragons to educated buyers, you're starting with the right mindset. If you're breeding for novelty, profit, or just curiosity, you may want to reconsider. Ethical breeding places animal welfare above all else.

Select Healthy, Mature Dragons

Only breed dragons that are:

- **At least 18 months old**
- **In peak health** with no signs of deformity, metabolic bone disease, or parasites
- **Genetically unrelated** to avoid inbreeding

Breeding unhealthy or immature dragons can result in weak clutches, increased birth defects, and high mortality.

Understand the Commitment

Each clutch can contain **20–30 eggs**, and females may lay **multiple clutches** from a single mating. That means you could be responsible for **50–100 hatchlings** in a single season. These babies require space, heat, lighting, food, and daily care—just like adults.

Before breeding:

- Have multiple enclosures ready
- Plan for feeding insects 3–5 times per day
- Budget for calcium, lighting, and vet care
- Consider how you'll **rehome** the hatchlings
- Unethical breeders often abandon or give away dragons without screening homes,

contributing to neglect and overpopulation.

Be Transparent with Buyers

If you're selling hatchlings, educate your buyers about:

- Proper enclosure size and lighting
- Dietary needs and supplementation
- Long-term care expectations

Avoid misleading people about a dragon's size, temperament, or rarity. Building trust through honesty helps prevent neglect and supports a healthier reptile community.

Commit to Lifelong Responsibility

Even after hatchlings leave your care, be open to questions, support, or even taking them back if needed. Ethical breeding doesn't end with the sale—it includes caring about where your dragons go and how they're treated.

Conclusion

Breeding bearded dragons is more than a project—it's a commitment to life. By approaching it with care, planning, and compassion, you help improve the lives of your animals and the future of the hobby. Responsible breeding starts with asking not just *Can I?* but *Should I?*—and following that answer with thoughtful action.

Part 11
Fun with Your Bearded Dragon

Chapter 49
Give Your Dragon a Name

One of the most exciting parts of bringing home a new pet is giving it a name. Your bearded dragon may be small now, but it deserves a name as big and bold as its personality! Whether your dragon is calm and curious or loves to run and explore, there's a perfect name out there waiting to be discovered.

This chapter will help you find a name that fits your dragon's look, behavior, or even something from your favorite books or movies. You'll also get fun name ideas, tips on picking the right one, and a special certificate at the end to make it official.

Fun Name Ideas by Theme

Color-Based Names

Your bearded dragon's color can be a great source of inspiration. Is your dragon orange, yellow, sandy, or dark brown? Check out these ideas:

For orange or red dragons:

- Ember
- Rusty
- Cheeto
- Flame
- Sunny

For yellow or gold dragons:

- Goldie
- Nugget
- Dandelion
- Buttercup
- Lemon

For white or pale dragons:

- Frost
- Snowball
- Pearl

- Marshmallow
- Ghost

For darker dragons:

- Shadow
- Ash
- Onyx
- Cocoa
- Stormy

Names Based on Behavior

Watch how your dragon acts for a few days. Does it run around? Climb everything? Or just love to chill under the heat lamp?

For energetic dragons:

- Dash
- Zippy
- Rocket
- Jumper
- Noodle

For laid-back dragons:

- Dozer
- Snooze
- Toast
- Pebble
- Slowpoke

For super curious dragons:

- Scout
- Gizmo
- Sniff

- Wiggles
- Blinky

Fantasy and Hero Names

Bearded dragons look like tiny dinosaurs or dragons from a fairytale. That makes fantasy names extra fun! Here are some magical and heroic ideas:

Fantasy-themed names:

- Draco
- Smaug
- Puff
- Saphira
- Falkor

Knight and hero names:

- Thor
- Zelda
- Arwen
- Merlin
- Luna

Tips for Choosing the Perfect Name

1. **Wait a few days.**

Watch your dragon's behavior before naming it. A name might come to you once you see how they move or what makes them special.

2. **Say it out loud.**

Try calling the name a few times. Does it sound fun? Is it easy to say?

3. **Be creative.**

You can mix two names (like "SpikeSpark" or "Toastianna") or make up a brand-new name that no one else has.

4. **Let your family help.**

Ask your parents, siblings, or friends to write down name ideas. Then vote on your favorite one together.

5. It's okay to change it.

If you pick a name and later find a better one, it's okay to switch. Your dragon won't mind at all.

Make It Official – Dragon Naming Certificate

Below is a special **Bearded Dragon Naming Certificate** you can fill out once you've chosen the perfect name. You can print this out and hang it on your wall or keep it near your dragon's enclosure!

🐉 Bearded Dragon Naming Certificate 🐉

This certifies that on this day, I have officially named my bearded dragon:

Name: ______________________________

Why I chose this name: ____________________________________

Chosen by: ____

Date: __________________________________

🐾 Welcome to the family, little dragon! 🐾

(Sign here with your name or a fancy dragon-keeper title!)

Conclusion

Your bearded dragon may not speak, but its name will be part of your bond from day one. A great name helps you connect, makes your dragon feel like part of the family, and adds a touch of fun and magic to your reptile journey.

So take your time, get inspired, and give your dragon a name that's as awesome, brave, silly, or legendary as they are!

Chapter 50
Bearded Dragon Personality Quiz

Every bearded dragon is a little different. Some are fast explorers who love to climb. Others are calm and relaxed, basking for hours without a care in the world. Some love their salads, and some would rather chase bugs all day. Wouldn't it be fun to figure out what kind of dragon personality your pet has?

This chapter includes a fun quiz to help you discover your bearded dragon's personality type. Is your dragon a Chill Sunbather, a Bold Explorer, or maybe a Curious Climber? Answer the questions below and tally your score to find out!

Take the Quiz: What Kind of Dragon Is Yours?

For each question, circle the answer that sounds most like your bearded dragon. Then we'll total up your points to reveal your dragon's personality.

1. When you open the enclosure, your dragon usually:

A. Stays still and watches you

B. Walks up to the glass or lifts its head

C. Starts climbing or pacing with excitement

2. During bath time, your dragon:

A. Just sits calmly in the water

B. Swims a little, then relaxes

C. Splashes, climbs, and tries to jump out

3. Your dragon's favorite activity seems to be:

A. Basking under the heat lamp

B. Exploring new things in the tank

C. Climbing on furniture or running around

4. When trying a new food, your dragon:

A. Ignores it at first and needs time

B. Looks at it, then decides to eat

C. Lunges or snatches it right away

5. How does your dragon act when handled?

A. Stays still or naps on you

B. Shifts around a bit but stays calm

C. Walks all over your arm or shoulder

6. When the tank is rearranged, your dragon:

A. Doesn't seem to notice

B. Slowly checks it out

C. Investigates every corner right away

7. What is your dragon's reaction to new people?

A. Stays in its spot and watches

B. Moves toward them with curiosity

C. Tries to climb out to meet them

Scoring Guide

- Mostly A answers = Chill Sunbather
- Mostly B answers = Curious Climber
- Mostly C answers = Bold Explorer

Your Dragon's Personality Type

Chill Sunbather 🐉☀️

Your dragon is calm, peaceful, and loves lounging in the warmth. They're easy to handle and enjoy a simple life of basking, eating, and watching the world go by. They're not easily startled, and they often make great companions for kids who enjoy a relaxed reptile.

Best activities:

- Gentle brushing or head rubs
- Lounging on your chest or shoulder
- Sunbathing in a safe window spot

Fun nickname ideas: Toast, Snoozer, Pebble, Dozer, Sunny

Curious Climber 🐉 🪵

Your dragon is always alert and always watching. They love to investigate their surroundings, try new foods, and explore new hiding spots. They may not be as hyper as a Bold Explorer, but they're definitely curious and intelligent. They enjoy a change of scenery and like figuring out new things.

Best activities:

- Rearranging tank decor
- Offering food puzzles or hanging greens
- Setting up a mini climbing wall inside the enclosure

Fun nickname ideas: Scout, Gizmo, Tinker, Maple, Wiggles

Bold Explorer 🐉 🚀

Your dragon is full of energy and adventure. They love climbing, running, exploring, and trying new things. They're bold, brave, and often the first to lunge at a new snack or leap onto your hand. They need lots of enrichment and love to explore outside their enclosure.

Best activities:

- Supervised floor time or outdoor time
- Climbing structures and tunnels
- Target training or food chase games

Fun nickname ideas: Dash, Rocket, Blaze, Noodle, Chaos

Personalize It: My Dragon's Profile

Fill this out for fun and post it near your dragon's tank!

My Dragon's Name: ______________________

Personality Type: ______________________

Favorite Food: ______________________

Favorite Activity: ______________________

What Makes My Dragon Unique: ____________________________________

What to Do With This Info?

Now that you know your dragon's personality, you can use it to:

- Choose better enrichment ideas
- Plan the perfect playtime routine
- Help your dragon feel more at home
- Pick the perfect dragon nickname
- Share fun facts with friends and family

Understanding your dragon's mood and behavior helps you take better care of them. It also shows that even though they're reptiles, bearded dragons have real personalities—just like you.

For Parents and Educators

This activity teaches observation, empathy, and responsibility. Encourage kids to retake the quiz as their dragon grows or after big changes in environment or behavior. They'll start to notice how animals adapt and how their bond can grow stronger over time.

Conclusion

Every dragon is different, and that's what makes caring for them so fun. Whether your beardie is a nap-loving Chill Sunbather or a wild and wiggly Bold Explorer, learning about their personality brings you closer together. Keep watching, keep learning, and enjoy the adventure of growing with your reptile friend.

Appendix
Bearded Dragon Age & Weight Chart
General Growth Guidelines
from Hatchling to Adult

This chart provides average size and weight benchmarks to help you track your bearded dragon's development. Growth rates may vary based on diet, lighting, health, and genetics, so use this as a general guide rather than a strict rule.

Age	Length (inches)	Weight (grams)	Growth Notes
0–2 months	3–7 inches	8–20 grams	Rapid growth; feeds multiple times daily
2–3 months	7–9 inches	20–40 grams	Strong appetite; should show steady increase in length
3–4 months	8–11 inches	40–80 grams	Begin introducing more greens; still insect-heavy diet
4–5 months	9–12 inches	80–120 grams	Active and alert; shedding frequently
5–6 months	11–16 inches	130–200 grams	Growth rate may begin to slow slightly
6–8 months	13–18 inches	200–280 grams	Shift diet to include more greens and vegetables
8–12 months	16–20 inches	250–400 grams	Approaching full size; more adult behavior noticeable
12–18 months	18–22 inches	350–500+ grams	Reaches adult size; feeding slows down
18+ months (Adult)	18–24 inches	400–600+ grams (varies)	Fully grown; maintain healthy weight with balanced diet

Note: Males tend to grow slightly larger and heavier than females. Sudden weight loss, stagnated growth, or excessive weight gain may signal health issues and should be discussed with a reptile vet.

Weekly Feeding Schedule

Here are **weekly feeding schedules by age** for bearded dragons, broken into three key life stages. Each includes guidance on insect frequency, vegetable variety, and supplement timing, all tailored to your dragon's nutritional needs at different phases of growth.

1. Hatchlings (0–2 Months)

Diet: 80–90% insects, 10–20% greens

Day	Insects (3–5 times daily)	Greens/Vegetables	Supplements
Monday	Tiny crickets or BSFL	Dandelion greens	Calcium without D3
Tuesday	Pinhead roaches	Mustard greens	Multivitamin
Wednesday	Crickets	Collard greens	Calcium without D3
Thursday	Black soldier fly larvae	Endive	Calcium without D3
Friday	Crickets + silkworm (optional)	Spring mix	Calcium with D3
Saturday	Roaches + BSFL	Turnip greens	Calcium without D3
Sunday	Crickets	Dandelion greens	No supplement

2. Juveniles (2–6 Months)

Diet: 70–80% insects, 20–30% greens

Day	Insects (2–3 times daily)	Greens/Vegetables	Supplements
Monday	Crickets or dubia roaches	Collard greens + shredded carrot	Calcium without D3
Tuesday	Black soldier fly larvae	Mustard greens + squash	Multivitamin
Wednesday	Crickets or silkworms	Dandelion greens	Calcium without D3
Thursday	Dubia roaches	Turnip greens + bell pepper	Calcium without D3
Friday	Hornworm (1–2) + crickets	Endive + zucchini	Calcium with D3
Saturday	Crickets or BSFL	Spring mix	Calcium without D3
Sunday	Roaches or BSFL	Collard greens	No supplement

3. Adults (12+ Months)

Diet: 70–80% greens, 20–30% insects

Day	Morning Salad	Insects (2–3 times/week)	Supplements
Monday	Mustard greens + squash	Dubia roaches (5–8)	Calcium without D3
Tuesday	Collard greens + bell pepper	None	Multivitamin
Wednesday	Dandelion greens + zucchini	Crickets (6–10)	Calcium without D3
Thursday	Turnip greens + green beans	None	No supplement
Friday	Spring mix + butternut squash	BSFL (5–7)	Calcium without D3
Saturday	Endive + shredded carrot	Optional hornworm (1–2)	Calcium with D3
Sunday	Collard greens + small fruit piece	None	No supplement

General Notes:

- **Insects** should be appropriately sized (no larger than the space between the dragon's eyes)
- **Dust insects** with supplements right before feeding
- **Greens** should be rotated weekly for variety
- Adjust portion sizes based on activity, appetite, and body condition
- Always provide fresh water and remove uneaten food daily

Let me know if you'd like printable versions or charts for display.

Get Your Free E-book

Get Your Free E-book
Scan the QR code below to instantly access the e-book
'The Ultimate Bearded Dragon Trivia Challenge', absolutely free

SCAN ME

https://bonus.grapevinebooks.com/bearded-trivia-challenge